GOLD

preliminary

PRELIMINARY ENGLISH TEST

coursebook

Clare Walsh

Lindsay Warwick

CONTENTS

Unit	Grammar	Vocabulary	Reading
1 Identity p. 6	Question forms p. 6 Indirect questions p. 12	Describing people p. 9 Deducing words in context p. 11	Matching (Part 2) *What does your profile photo say about you?* p. 10
2 The business of food p. 14	Present simple and continuous p.18 Modals of possibility p. 20	Collocations: food p. 14 Suffixes: *-ful, -ly, -less, -ment, -able* p. 17	Four-option multiple choice (Part 4) *The tricks of food photographers* p. 16
Progress Test 1 p. 22			
3 Mind your manners p. 24	*-ing* forms and infinitives p. 27 Modals of obligation p. 30	Phrasal verbs p. 25 Describing feelings p. 26	True/False (Part 3) *Mobile manners* p. 28
4 Leaving a record p. 32	Present perfect and past simple p. 34 *used to* p. 37	Linking words: addition and contrast p. 33 Town and city p. 38	Four-option multiple-choice cloze (Part 5) *New technology finds old history* p. 32
Progress Test 2 p. 40			
5 Swap it p. 42	Comparatives and superlatives p. 45 *too* and *enough, so* and *such* p. 48	Verbs related to clothes p. 42 Order of adjectives p. 43 House and home p. 47	Matching (Part 2) *Holiday home exchange* p. 46
6 You live and learn p. 50	Past simple and past continuous p. 52 Past perfect simple p. 56	Prepositional phrases p. 51 Education p. 53	Four-option multiple choice (Part 4) *English dot com* p. 50
Progress test 3 p. 58			
7 Water p. 60	Countable and uncountable nouns p. 61 Articles p. 66	Weather p. 62 Adjectives + prepositions p. 64	True/False (Part 3) *New Forest Health Spa* p. 64
8 Celebrity p. 68	Reported speech p. 72 Reported questions p. 74	Entertainment p. 69 *-ed* and *-ing* adjectives p. 71	Four-option multiple-choice cloze (Part 5) *The woman whose life is a brand* p. 70
Progress test 4 p. 76			
9 Creativity p. 78	Modals of ability p. 79 Relative clauses p. 83	Formal language p. 81 Job skills p. 84 Prefixes p. 84	Matching (Part 2) *Photography courses* p. 80
10 What's it worth? p. 86	Passive voice p. 87 *get/have something done* p. 89	Shops and services p. 88 Verbs and prepositions p. 91	Three-option multiple choice (Part 1) *The sales* p. 90
Progress test 5 p. 94			
11 A small world p. 96	Future forms p. 100 *will* and *going to* p. 102	Compound adjectives p. 97 Travel and transport p. 98	Four-option mutiple choice (Part 4) *The jungle town lost to tourists* p. 96
12 Extreme p. 104	Zero and first conditionals p. 105 Second conditional p. 108	Confusing words p. 107 Sport and leisure p. 110	Three-option multiple choice (Part 1) *Danger* p. 106
Progress Test 6 p. 112			

Exam information p. 4   **Communication activities** p. 114   **Grammar reference** p. 124

Listening	Speaking	Writing
Multiple choice (Part 1) Short recordings p. 8	Personal questions (Part 1) *Identity* p. 7	Informal letter (Part 3) Organising your work in paragraphs p. 13
Multiple choice (Part 2) *Shopping on the go* p. 19	Extended turn (Part 3) and General conversation (Part 4) *Where food comes from* p. 15	Story (Part 3) Using time linkers p. 21
True/False (Part 4) *Make new friends with the Supper Club* p. 26	Extended turn (Part 3) and General conversation (Part 4) *Disagreements* p. 24	Message (Part 2) Using functional phrases p. 31
Multiple choice (Part 1) Short recordings p. 36	Simulated situation (Part 2) *Personal objects* p. 35	Sentence transformations (Part 1) Finding the language that's being tested p. 39
Gap-fill (Part 3) *Valley University car share scheme* p. 44	Extended turn (Part 3) and General conversation (Part 4) *Swapping clothes* p. 43	Message (Part 2) Following the task instructions p. 49
True/False (Part 4) *Starting out* p. 54	Personal questions (Part 1) *Teaching new skills to young people* p. 55	Story (Part 3) Using narrative tenses p. 57
Multiple choice (Part 2) *Top cruises with Ocean Star* p. 60	Simulated situation (Part 2) *Extreme races* p. 63	Informal letter (Part 3) Editing your work p. 67
Gap-fill (Part 3) *The New York Reality TV School* p. 73	Extended turn (Part 3) and General conversation (Part 4) *Entertainment* p. 69	Story (Part 3) Structuring your paragraphs p. 75
Multiple choice (Part 2) *The power of gaming* p. 82	Extended turn (Part 3) *Lee Hadwin's art* p. 78	Sentence transformations (Part 1) Checking your spelling p. 85
Gap-fill (Part 3) *Charity Auction Evening* p. 86	Simulated situation (Part 2) *Gifts* p. 92	Note (Part 2) Joining sentences with linkers p. 93
Multiple choice (Part 1) Short recordings p. 99	Extended turn (Part 3) and General conversation (Part 4) *People and animals* p. 101	Informal letter (Part 3) Using informal linkers p. 103
True/False (Part 4) *We're all good at something…* p. 105	Simulated situation (Part 2) *Travelling in New Zealand* p.109	Sentence transformations (Part 1) Keeping the meanings the same p. 111

Writing reference p. 133   **Functions bank** p. 152   **Exam focus** p. 156

Exam information

The *Cambridge English: Preliminary* exam is made up of three papers, each testing a different area of ability in English. *Paper 1: Reading and Writing* is worth 50 percent of the total mark. *Paper 2: Listening* and *Paper 3: Speaking* are each worth 25 percent of the total mark.

Paper 1: Reading and Writing (1 hour 30 minutes)

Paper 1 has two sections. The Reading section has five parts (35 questions) and is worth 25 percent of the final exam mark. The Writing section has three parts and is also worth 25 percent of the final exam mark. Each part tests different reading and writing skills.

Reading

Part 1 Three-option multiple-choice	Focus	Reading real-world notices and short texts for the main message
	Task	Questions 1–5. Choose the correct answer from three possible options for each of five very short texts (e.g. notices, emails).
Part 2 Matching	Focus	Scanning for detail
	Task	Questions 6–10. Read descriptions of five people, then match each person's requirements to one of eight short texts.
Part 3 True/False	Focus	Scanning for specific information and ignoring information that is not useful
	Task	Questions 11–20. Read a text which provides information (e.g. a brochure or website), and decide whether ten statements are correct or incorrect.
Part 4 Four-option multiple-choice	Focus	Reading for detail; understanding attitude and opinion; reading for gist and global meaning
	Task	Questions 21–25. Read one long text and answer five multiple-choice questions about it.
Part 5 Four-option multiple-choice cloze	Focus	Vocabulary/Lexico-grammatical
	Task	Questions 26–35. Complete a short text with text gaps, by choosing the correct word from four possible answers for each gap.

Writing

Part 1 Sentence transformations	Focus	Grammar and vocabulary
	Task	Questions 1–5. Read five pairs of sentences and complete the gap in the second sentence so that it means the same as the first.
Part 2 Short communicative message	Focus	Giving information, thanking, apologising, warning, inviting, suggesting, giving advice, arranging a meeting, etc.
	Task	Write a short message, e.g. an email, including the three things mentioned in the task. Write between 35 and 45 words.
Part 3 Longer piece of continuous writing	Focus	Respond to news, describe something, give advice, make suggestions, etc.
	Task	Choose one of two tasks and write around 100 words. You can either reply to a letter from a friend, or write a story using the title or the first line you are given.

Paper 2: Listening (approximately 30 minutes)

The Listening Paper has four parts, with a total of 25 questions. It is worth 25 percent of the final mark. You hear each recording twice.		
Part 1 **Multiple choice (discrete)**	*Focus*	Listening for detail
	Task	Questions 1–7. Listen to seven short recordings and, for each one, choose the correct picture out of three options.
Part 2 **Multiple choice**	*Focus*	Listening for specific information and detailed meaning
	Task	Questions 8–13. Listen to a talk or interview and then choose the correct answer from three possible options.
Part 3 **Gap-fill**	*Focus*	Listening for detail
	Task	Questions 14–19. Listen to someone giving information and complete six gaps in a page of notes.
Part 4 **True/False**	*Focus*	Listening for detailed information and understanding people's attitudes or opinions
	Task	Questions 20–25. Listen to a conversation and decide whether six statements are true or false.

Paper 3: Speaking (10–12 minutes)

The Speaking Test is worth 25 percent of the final mark. It has four parts. You take the Speaking Test with another candidate, and there will be two examiners. One examiner asks the questions and the other examiner just listens.		
Part 1 **Personal questions** (2–3 minutes)	*Focus*	Giving personal and factual information about your life; answering questions about your past, present, and future
	Task	Answer the examiner's questions about your present situation, past experiences and future plans.
Part 2 **Simulated situation** (2–3 minutes)	*Focus*	Making suggestions and recommendations; giving opinions and coming to an agreement
	Task	Look at the set of pictures and discuss a situation that the examiner gives you.
Part 3 **Extended turn** (3 minutes)	*Focus*	Describing a picture with appropriate vocabulary
	Task	Talk about a photograph for about one minute, and listen to your partner's description of a different photograph. Both photos will be about the same topic.
Part 4 **General conversation** (3 minutes)	*Focus*	Discussing personal likes, dislikes, preferences and opinions, giving reasons where necessary; continuing a discussion
	Task	Discuss a question or questions with your partner. The question(s) will be on the same topic as the photographs in Part 3.

For more information, see the **Writing reference** (page 133) and the **Exam focus** (page 156).

Identity

1

Speaking

1 **Work in pairs and discuss the questions.**

1 What's your name? How did you get that name?
2 Does your name have a special meaning in your country?
3 Do you like your name? Why/Why not?

Reading

2 **You are going to read an article called *What's in a name?* What do you think the question means? Read the text to find out if you are right.**

Front page | National | International | Financial

12:47 | 100%

Wednesday 12 | Issues **Sections** Settings

What's in a name?

More and more parents are choosing unusual names for their children. **Have unusual names appeared only recently?** Well, no. We have records from the United States in the nineteenth and early twentieth centuries of children named Post Office, Garage Empty and Nice Carr. **How does your name affect your life?**

Well, people will behave differently towards you, for a start. In one test, teachers gave better marks to work with the 'normal' names Karen and David at the top, and lower marks to the same piece of work with the less popular names of Hubert and Bertha. You might behave differently, too. Scientists have found that the first letters of your name affect your choices in life. People called Omar are more likely to move to Omaha or vote for Obama. There are more Phils in Philadelphia and lawyers named Larry and Laura. **Who knows the reasons for this?** Scientists are still trying to understand it.

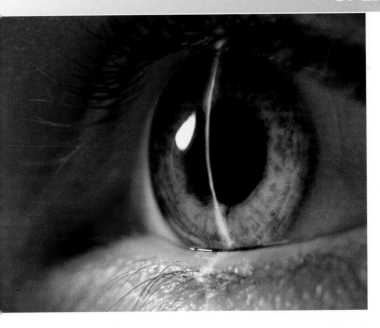

3 **Read the text again and answer the questions.**

1 How can a less popular name affect someone?

2 Why are the first letters of your name important?

4 **Work in pairs. How might a name change the way we think about a person?**

Question forms

▶ **GRAMMAR** REFERENCE p.124

5 **Look at the bold questions in the article** *What's in a name?* **and write them in the correct place in the chart.**

yes/no questions

auxiliary	subject	main verb + the rest
Do (1)	you (2)	like your name? (3) ....

wh- object questions

question word	auxiliary	subject	main verb + the rest
How (4)	did (5)	you (6)	get that name? (7) ....

wh- subject questions

question word	main verb	the rest
Who (8)	gave (9)	you that name? (10) ....

6 ▶ 01 **You are going to hear two people meeting for the first time. What's the girl's name? Is it an unusual name everywhere?**

7 **Look at the answers from the conversation in Activity 6. What were the questions?**

1 **A:** ....
  B: D-E-S-T-I-N-Y, just like the word.

2 **A:** ....
  B: Just on vacation.

3 **A:** ....
  B: My mom did.

4 **A:** ....
  B: My mom says she was just really happy when I arrived.

5 **A:** ....
  B: Yeah, it was my grandpa's name.

8 **Listen again and check your answers to Activity 7.**

9 **Work in pairs and discuss the questions.**

1 Imagine that you had to choose a new name. What would you choose? Why?

2 What other things give you a sense of identity?

Speaking

Personal questions (Part 1)

▶ **FUNCTIONS** BANK p.152

10 ▶ 02 **Listen to the two students giving answers to Part 1 of the Speaking test. Who gives better answers? Why?**

11 **Take turns to ask each other questions. Ask at least two questions about**

1 work or studies.

2 free time.

3 where you live.

4 learning English.

Listening
Multiple choice (Part 1)

1 **Work in pairs. Look at the first set of pictures in Activity 4 and answer the questions.**

1 What does the girl look like in each picture?
2 What do the pictures have in common? What makes them different?

2 ▶ **03 In Part 1, there are seven questions. For each question, there are three pictures and a short recording. Listen to the first half of the recording for question 1 in Activity 4. What information do you learn about the girl?**

3 ▶ **04 Now listen to the whole recording.**

1 Which photo shows the girl's sister?
2 What information gives you the answer?

> **EXAM TIP**
>
> In Listening Part 1, the answer may come at the beginning, in the middle or at the end of the recording. Often you need to listen to the whole recording to get the correct answer.

4 ▶ **05 Now listen to recordings 2–7. For each question, choose the correct picture.**

1 What does the girl's sister look like?

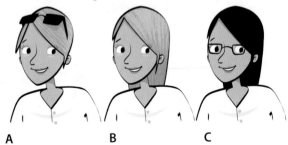

A   B   C

2 What's already in the suitcase?

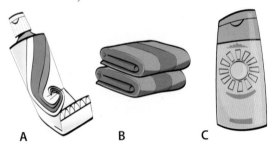

A   B   C

3 What is the woman going to buy?

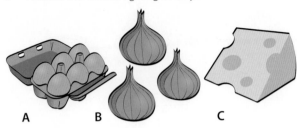

A   B   C

4 What did the man do on holiday?

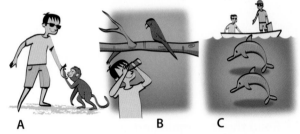

A   B   C

5 What will the weather be like tomorrow morning?

A   B   C

6 Who does the boy think should win the competition?

A   B   C

7 Where will the girl go first?

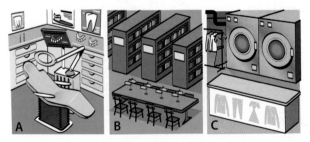

A   B   C

5 **Work in pairs and discuss the questions.**

1 Where can you find short conversations like these to practise listening to?
2 Do you think it's important to understand every word when you listen? Why/Why not?

Reading

1 Work in pairs and discuss the questions.

1 What kind of people do you like spending time with? Why?

2 What kind of person do you think makes a good work colleague? Why?

2 Read about the big five character types and follow the instructions.

The big five character types

Many scientists now believe that there are only five main types of character. Which one are you? Do our quiz on page 114 to find out.

RESULTS

Open people are **curious** and like art and adventure. They have unusual beliefs which some people think are **strange**.

Conscientious people are **organised and ambitious**, but never make quick decisions. They are **reliable and punctual**.

Extroverted people are **cheerful** and love doing exciting things. They have energy, talk a lot and are never **shy**.

Anxious people are **sensitive**. They care about details and want to get things right. Sometimes they get a bit **nervous**.

Agreeable people are friendly and **generous**. They believe that everyone is good and **honest**.

3 Work in pairs. Are your strongest character types the same? Do you both agree there are five main character types?

Describing people

4 Complete the email. Choose from the adjectives in bold from Activity 2.

To: Jo@aol-online.com
From: Jemma@hotmail.com

Anyway, you asked to see a photo of my family so here it is. Mum and Dad are both middle-aged now but Dad's the overweight, bald one! He used to have a beard that I hated. We're very different from each other. He's (**1**) punctual. I'm always late. He plans everything and is (**2**) organised. I'm not! He loves talking to people but I'm (**3**) shy. Mum's always smartly dressed and (**4**) sensitive – she always has a smile on her face. She's (**5**) reliable honest so always does what she promises to do. She's also really (**6**) honest and will tell you exactly what she thinks! My brother Ryan's in his teens. He's only medium-height but he's well-built for his age and good-looking. He's (**7**) ambitious and wants to be a Formula 1 engineer one day. He's (**8**) sensitive too, so he always knows when I'm feeling a bit sad. Girls love him!

5 Look at the underlined words/phrases in the email. Do they describe age, looks or size?

Speaking

6 Work in pairs and discuss the questions.

1 Which family member and friend are you most similar to?

2 Which family member and friend are you most different from?

Speaking

1 **Work in pairs and discuss the questions.**

1 Do you have a social networking profile photo? Why/Why not?

2 How important do you think a person's profile photo is? Why?

3 What kind of person do you think the man in the photo is?

Phil Stevens

| Profile | Friends | Networks |

Organise | Upload | Profile | Photos | Videos

Phil Stevens
- Studied at the University of Exeter
- Works at AWC engineering
- Lives in Torbay
- Single
- Born on 17 April

Phil Stevens is now friends with ***Charlotte Hawkins***.
An hour ago

Phil Stevens: On my way to the beach. Can't wait!
20 May

Phil Stevens wants to invite **you** to a beach party on 28 May.
20 May

Phil Stevens likes ***Carmen Caligari's*** status.
19 May

Reading
Matching (Part 2)

2 **The people below want to choose a profile photo for a social networking site. Read their profiles and underline the key pieces of information in each.**

1 Jacob likes moving around the country and learning to do interesting things he's never done before. He is proud of his many artistic and sporting talents.

2 Naomi finds her work very stressful. She has a good imagination and spends a lot of time thinking about living in a more relaxing place.

3 Laura's active and loves having fun. However, she doesn't like rules and often gets into trouble for breaking them.

4 Kasia loves her boyfriend very much. She wants to get married to him in the future. She hopes that they will grow old together.

5 Marcus enjoys teaching at a primary school. His students say he always listens to them carefully. He and his wife really want to have their own children one day.

What does your profile photo say about you?

A With an animal

A photo with an animal shows that you can care for people. It is important for you to give these people your full attention so you can help them develop. It can also mean that you enjoy taking care of plants and other living things, or that you have a strong need to be a parent.

B Dancing

Dancing in a photo says you are lively and always looking for pleasure. Dancing is connected with feeling free so you probably don't do what you should do all the time. This might cause problems for you sometimes.

C With a partner

This photo tells everyone that you have found a special person that you care for. It says that you are in a serious relationship with that person, and you want to be together for a long time. You are looking for something deeper in life.

D With a man/woman who is just a friend

A photo with a friend of the same sex shows that you are a talented storyteller. You love having fun and playing jokes on people. You enjoy relationships with people and always want to know what other people are doing.

E Doing an activity

This photo says that you think your many creative and athletic abilities are important. You care a lot about experiences and often try new and exciting activities. You don't want to stay in the same place for too long and you're possibly not looking for a serious relationship at the moment.

F Looking away from the camera

This photo says you want to be different from other people. You are confident about making your own decisions. You are independent so no one can stop you doing what you want! You like spending time alone in thought.

G On holiday

A holiday photo could say that you are a dreamer. It suggests you worry a lot about things in your job and at home. You probably dream of moving to an area where your worries have gone and your life is carefree.

H On a night out with friends

This image shows that you enjoy your social life very much. You love talking and are at your happiest when other people pay you a lot of attention.

3 Read about eight different profile photos and what they say about a person. Which one is most suitable for Jacob? Why?

EXAM TIP

Underline the key information requirements in the people descriptions. Then read the eight texts carefully and underline any information that matches.

4 Which type of photograph A–H is most suitable for the other people in Activity 2?

Vocabulary

Deducing words in context

5 Look at these words/phrases from the text. Which meaning is correct for each one, A or B?

LANGUAGE TIP

You don't need to understand every word in a text. If you see a word that you don't know, try to guess the meaning by looking at the words around it.

1 *connected with* (section B)
  A has a relationship with
  B is a part of something

2 *a serious relationship* (section C)
  A involved closely with someone
  B a friendship with no laughter

3 *talented* (section D)
  A not skilled
  B very good at

4 *independent* (section F)
  A do things without any help
  B get nervous very easily

5 *dreamer* (section G)
  A a person that is not real
  B a person who has impossible plans and ideas.

Speaking

6 Work in pairs and discuss the questions.

1 According to the article, which photo would be most suitable for you?

2 Is it possible to look at a picture of someone and know what kind of person they are? Why/Why not?

Speaking

1 Work in pairs and discuss the questions.

1 When was the last time you met someone new? What did you chat about?

2 What information do people usually give about themselves to someone they've just met?

Listening

2 ▶ 06 Listen to a radio programme about meeting people for the first time. What is the reporter, Melanie, trying to find out? How many people does she speak to?

3 Listen again and answer the questions.

1 Which topics are not popular?

2 How do the people respond to questions they don't want to answer?

4 Complete the questions with the words in brackets in the correct order. Then listen and check.

1 Have you any idea *if there is a* toilet in here? (a / if / there's)

2 Could you tell me *where I can* get a drink? (can / I / where)

3 What *do you do* for a living? (do / do / you)

4 Would you mind *telling me how much* you earn? (how much / me / telling)

5 Do you know *if it is okay* for me to sit here? (if / okay / it's)

6 *Have you got* a girlfriend or are you single? (got / have / you)

5 Work in pairs and discuss the questions.

1 What topics should you never talk about when you first meet someone in your country?

2 Are there any situations where it's okay to talk about these topics?

Indirect questions

▶ **GRAMMAR** REFERENCE p.124

6 Look at the questions 1–6 in Activity 4 and answer the questions.

1 Which of the questions in Activity 4 are direct and which are indirect?

2 Are direct questions or indirect questions more polite?

3 How is the word order different in an indirect question?

4 With indirect questions, do you need an auxiliary such as *do* or *can*?

5 When do we use *if* or *whether* in an indirect question?

6 Which words do you think are stressed in Activity 4 questions 1–6?

LANGUAGE TIP

Use indirect questions when you're asking difficult questions and want to be more polite, or if you're not sure that the listener knows the answer. *Can I ask if that's your natural hair colour? Could you tell me whether this train stops at Cheltenham?*

7 Complete the indirect questions so they mean the same as the direct questions. Use no more than three words.

1 Are you married or single?
Can you tell me *if you are* married or single?

2 Where do you live?
I'd like to know *where you* live.

3 Do you pay a lot of rent?
Would you mind telling me *if you pay* a lot of rent?

4 How much do you weigh?
Do you know *how much you* weigh?

5 How do you spend your weekends?
Can you tell me *how you spend* your weekends?

6 How old are you?
I'd like to know how *old you are*.

7 What do you do for a living?
Would you mind telling me *what you do* for a living?

8 How much do you earn?
Could you tell me how *much you earn*?

Speaking

8 Work in different pairs. Imagine you are classmates who have just met. What information is your partner happy to give you? Use questions from Activity 4 to help you.

Speaking

1 **Look at quotes A–C from the children of rock stars, then discuss the questions.**

1 Would you like to have a famous parent? Why/Why not?

2 Would you prefer to have a sports star, a musician, or an actor for a parent? Why?

A 'Friends, friends' mothers, kids, all different people come up to me pretty much every day to say "Oh we love your dad."'
Liv Tyler talking about her dad, Aerosmith singer Steven Tyler.

B 'It wasn't until I was in high school that I realised that not everyone's dad put on makeup and wielded a snake!'
Calico Cooper talking about her dad, Alice Cooper.

C 'So, he's wearing leather pants and a feather boa, but he would be like, "Did you do your chores today?" or, "That dress is too short!"'
Zoe Kravitz talking about her dad, Lenny Kravitz.

Writing

Informal letter (Part 3)

▶ **WRITING** REFERENCE p.134

▶ **FUNCTIONS** BANK p.154

2 **Look at the exam task and underline what you have to do.**

> This is part of an email you receive from an English friend, Becky.
>
> > *So, that's what my family are like. In your next letter, perhaps you could tell me a bit about someone in your family. What are they like?*
>
> Now write a letter to Becky, answering her question. Write your **letter** in about **100 words**.

3 **Read Eva's reply to Becky and answer the questions. Then compare your answers in pairs.**

1 What's unusual about Eva's dad?

2 What do we learn about Eva's dad from her letter?

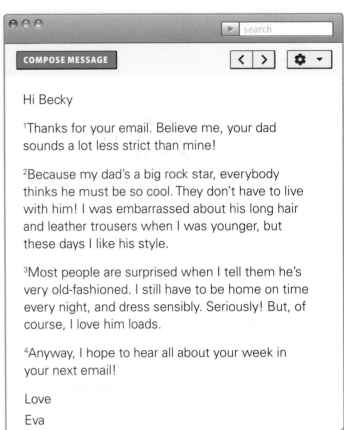

Hi Becky

[1]Thanks for your email. Believe me, your dad sounds a lot less strict than mine!

[2]Because my dad's a big rock star, everybody thinks he must be so cool. They don't have to live with him! I was embarrassed about his long hair and leather trousers when I was younger, but these days I like his style.

[3]Most people are surprised when I tell them he's very old-fashioned. I still have to be home on time every night, and dress sensibly. Seriously! But, of course, I love him loads.

[4]Anyway, I hope to hear all about your week in your next email!

Love

Eva

4 **Look at Eva's letter again. Match paragraphs 1–4 with the main ideas A–D.**

A describing personality

B talking about what Becky said in her letter

C talking about future contact with Becky

D describing looks

EXAM TIP

When you write a longer piece of writing, you MUST write complete sentences and organise your work into three or four paragraphs, with one theme per paragraph.

5 **Look at the sample answer on page 114. Where should the paragraph breaks be?**

6 **Write your letter to Becky. Don't forget to write about 100 words and use paragraphs.**

The business of food

2

Listening

1 **Work in pairs and discuss the questions.**

1 Who buys food in your home? How much time do you spend planning and preparing meals?

2 What's most important to you when you buy food: cost, health benefits or where it comes from? Why?

2 ▶ 07 **You will hear part of a radio interview with a woman called Sue, who has written a book about where food comes from. Listen and tick (✓) the words you hear.**

fish	fruit	rice	juice	chips	sausage	alcohol
meat	salt	vegetables		potatoes	sugar	

3 **Listen again and answer the questions.**

1 What changes to our food habits does Sue mention?

2 What problems with food labels does she describe?

3 Who does Sue think suffers because of these problems?

LANGUAGE TIP

In your vocabulary notebook, make sections for different topics (food, transport and travel, etc.). It will make it easier to learn new words and use them again.

Vocabulary

Collocations: food

4 **Match words 1–7 from the radio interview with the meanings A–G.**

1	fresh ingredients	A	cooked quickly by moving it around in hot oil
2	local speciality	B	containing a lot of butter or oil
3	stir-fried (vegetables)	C	containing no alcohol
4	raw (fish)	D	a well-known dish from a particular area
5	soft drinks	E	limiting the amount you eat to get thinner
6	fatty (food)	F	recently picked and prepared
7	on a diet	G	cooked in water
8	boiled (rice)	H	uncooked, particularly when a food is usually eaten cooked

5 Complete the questions with a word or words from Activity 4.

1 Do you prefer food made with frozen or .... ?

2 What is your favourite .... from your region?

3 Do you drink fizzy .... ? Do you think they're healthy/unhealthy?

4 Have you ever eaten .... fish or meat? Do you prefer it cooked?

5 Do people eat less .... food, like cake, these days?

6 Would it be easy for you to go .... and stop eating unhealthy food?

7 Do people from your region eat more chips or .... potatoes?

8 What's your favourite sauce with .... vegetables? Do you often cook this way?

6 Discuss the questions in Activity 5 in pairs.

Speaking
Extended turn (Part 3)

7 Have you ever tried to grow your own fruit or vegetables, or catch your own food? What did you enjoy/not enjoy about the experience?

8 ▶ 08 Listen to two students describing the photographs on this page.

1 What do the two students have to do?

2 How long do they have to speak for?

3 Did the students have enough to say?

9 Listen again. What things do Daniela and Alejandro describe? Could they describe more?

10 Work in pairs. Student A turn to page 115. Student B, turn to page 116. Follow the instructions.

Work in pairs. Student A turn to page 115. Student B, turn to page 116.

EXAM TIP

When you describe your photo, imagine you are speaking to someone who cannot see it. This will help you describe it clearly.

General conversation (Part 4)

11 ▶ 09 In Part 4 of the Speaking test, you will be asked to discuss the general theme of the photographs. Listen to Part 4. Who said these things? Write A for Alejandro or D for Daniela.

1 I lived near a farm.

2 I've been fishing.

3 I hate going to the supermarket.

4 I order some food products on the internet.

12 Work in pairs. Talk together about the food that you like for two or three minutes. Use the ideas below to help you.

1 your favourite food as a child

2 your favourite food now

3 the food you dislike

4 the kinds of food you usually eat

Speaking

1 **Work in pairs and discuss the questions.**

1 Would you like to eat the meal in the photo? Why/Why not?

2 What skills do you need to make this meal? Could you do it?

3 What skills do you need to be able to photograph food like this?

Reading
Multiple choice (Part 4)

2 **Work in pairs. Read the headline. What tricks do you think the article is about?**

3 **Read the text and answer the questions.**

1 Were your predictions correct?

2 Why do you think the writer wrote this text? Who did he write it for?

▶ Food photography

RECIPES
CHEFS
PROGRAMMES
INGREDIENTS
TECHNIQUES
BLOG
FAQ

The tricks of food photographers

We've all seen the **gorgeous** photos of **colourful** vegetables and **freshly-**baked cakes in books and magazines. When we see these pictures we believe that if we follow the recipe, we can make food that looks like that too. However, not many people realise the strange things that photographers use to change a simple plate of food into the mouth-watering dishes in the photos.

Food is one of the most difficult subjects for photographers. Hot food goes cold, cold food goes dry, and frozen food melts, making it **useless**. But don't worry, because food photographers have the tools to deal with these problems. They don't just visit photography shops. They also visit art shops, garages and pharmacies. As well as camera **equipment**, a photographer's bag includes motor oil to help sauces look brighter, hairspray to stop cakes looking dry, and a **spoonful** of shoe polish to help meat look cooked.

There are a few rules about food that photographers have to follow. If a photo is going to become part of an advert, rules say the food which the company wants to advertise must be the real thing. However, any other food in the photo doesn't need to be real. Plastic 'fruit' or glass 'ice' in a drink next to the real dessert is **acceptable**, according to the rules. Of course, there are some photographers who choose not to use non-food items in their photos, even when the rules allow it, but that does make their job much more challenging.

Whether a food photographer believes in using tricks or not, one thing is definitely true: food photography needs a lot of patience.

◀ ▶

4 **Read the text again. For each question choose the correct answer, A–D.**

> **EXAM TIP**
>
> Make sure you read the text carefully at least twice to be able to answer question 1 (the writer's purpose) and question 5 (the meaning of the whole text).

1 What is the writer trying to do in the text?

 A advise photographers how to take photos of food
 B explain how photographers take photos of food
 C encourage people to become food photographers
 D describe a day in his life as a food photographer

2 The writer says that people who read cookbooks

 A choose them because of the gorgeous photos.
 B examine the look of the photos too closely.
 C dislike the practice of using perfect photos.
 D think their own food will look like the photos.

3 What are the rules about food advertising?

 A All the food in the advert must be the real thing.
 B Only the food being advertised needs to be real.
 C Plastic food cannot be seen anywhere in a photo.
 D Photographers must be open about their techniques.

4 The writer thinks that using plastic food is

 A a dishonest technique to use.
 B an easier option for photographers.
 C an interesting tool to employ.
 D necessary for food to look nice.

5 What might the writer say to a friend?

> **A** I'm pleased that some photographers refuse to use these techniques with food.

> **B** I'm worried by the small number of photographers who can take good food photos.

> **C** I'm sure that only creative people have the skill to become a good photographer.

> **D** I'm amazed by the products that professionals use to make their photos look real.

Speaking

5 **Work in pairs. Turn to page 115.**

6 **Work in pairs and discuss the questions.**

1 Do you agree with the use of tricks in food photography? Why/Why not?

2 Which trick do you dislike the most? Why?

3 How has this article changed your views on food advertising?

Vocabulary

Suffixes

7 **Complete the sentences with a word in bold from the text in Activity 2.**

1 I don't think it's ever .... to use motor oil in food photos.

2 Professional photographers have a lot of expensive ....

3 Please put a .... of sugar in my tea.

4 This knife won't cut anything. It's .... !

5 I've got red, orange and yellow peppers. Don't they look .... ?

6 I love the smell of ....-baked bread.

> **LANGUAGE TIP**
>
> Add a suffix to the end of a word to change its form, e.g. from a noun to an adjective. Sometimes the suffix changes the meaning of the word, e.g. *-ful* (full of/a quantity of), *-less* (without) and *-able* (can).

8 **Complete the words in the sentences with an appropriate suffix.**

1 If I go to the supermarket when I'm hungry, I buy an arm...... of cakes.

2 I sometimes have a microwave...... meal when I'm in a hurry.

3 I often burn food when I cook. I'm so care...... !

4 I love spicy food. Any other food is taste...... to me.

5 I'm hope...... that someone will cook me dinner later tonight.

6 Fresh coffee in the morning smells wonder...... .

7 I hate restaurants with live entertain...... .

8 I like food you can prepare quick...... .

9 **Work in pairs. Are the sentences in Activity 8 true for you? Why/Why not?**

Reading

1 Work in pairs. Look at the photo. What do you think the woman is doing? What do you think she does for a living?

2 Read the text. Were your predictions correct?

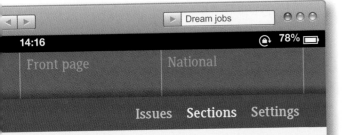

DREAM JOBS ice cream taster

This is Michaela. (**1**) She's tasting ice cream **B** flavours for a food company. She's 20, (**2**) lives in Brighton and **usually** (**3**) attends classes on food technology at college, but this summer (**4**) she's working as an ice cream taster. **D**

'Most of my friends (**5**) believe it's the best job in the world', says Michaela, 'They think all I do is eat ice cream all day, but it's hard work. I'm **always** in the factory from 8 a.m. to 6 p.m. and to

taste the ice cream, you (**6**) put just a little in your mouth. I don't **often** eat more than a litre a week.

So, does Michaela love ice cream? 'I don't mind it. I have it a **few times a year** but to be honest I prefer chips!'

Present simple and continuous

▶ **GRAMMAR** REFERENCE p.124

3 Match the uses of the present simple and present continuous A–F with examples 1–6 in Activity 2.

A A regular repeated action (*present simple*)

B A permanent situation (*present simple*)

C Spoken instructions and processes (*present simple*)

D With stative verbs (*present simple*)

E An action happening at this exact time (*present continuous*)

F A temporary situation happening around this time (*present continuous*)

> **LANGUAGE TIP**
>
> Stative verbs describe a state, e.g. *know, agree, believe*. We don't usually use them in the present continuous form.

4 Look at the adverbs in bold in Activity 2 and answer the questions.

1 Do the adverbs of frequency come

   A before or after an auxiliary verb?

   B before or after the verb *to be*?

   C before or after all other verbs?

2 Do longer adverbial phrases come at the beginning or end of a sentence?

5 Read the text. Would you like this job? Why/Why not? Tell a partner.

DREAM JOBS food guide

Fred (**1**) works....... (*work*) as a food guide for a travel company. Each month he (**2**) takes....... (*take*) people who (**3**) .....want..... (*want*) to learn about Asian food around Vietnam or Thailand. At the moment he (**4**) is visiting (*visit*) Hanoi with ten   British tourists.

Fred's an expert in Asian cookery. He already speaks Vietnamese and (**5**) is learning (*learn*) to speak Thai in his free time. During his tours he (**6**) .....teaches.... (*teach*) the group how to cook local food. Today he (**7**) is showing (*show*) them a popular market.

Fred (**8**) thinks..... (*think*) his job is great. 'I (**9**) don't often see (*not/often/see*) my friends and family but I meet interesting people and see amazing places. I (**10**) am having (*have*) the time of my life!'

6 Put the verbs in brackets from Activity 5 into the correct present simple or continuous form.

5 ▶ 12 **Now read through questions 2–7 and underline the keywords. Then listen to the whole recording and choose the best answers.**

1 When Magda first heard about the supermarket, she thought it
   A would be interesting.
   B sounded unpleasant.
   C was a practical idea.

2 Magda says the supermarket is unusual because it
   A uses mobile phones.
   B delivers food quickly.
   C looks like a normal supermarket.

3 What did Magda buy in the supermarket?
   A drinks
   B vegetables
   C shampoo

4 Magda thinks the supermarket works well in South Korea because South Koreans
   A don't have much free time.
   B like new technology.
   C have to wait a long time for transport.

5 Why did Magda like the new supermarket?
   A It was easy to use.
   B It was cheap.
   C It was fun.

6 Magda says that the Korean people
   A welcomed the new shop.
   B were unsure about using it.
   C preferred other supermarkets.

7 Magda thinks that in Britain, this type of shop would
   A be too expensive.
   B not be technically possible.
   C be unpopular with the people.

Vocabulary

1 **Look at the phrases in the box. Do they relate to photo A, photo B or both?**

shop online   special deals   see the quality
scan a product   deliver the products

2 **The photos show different ways to buy food. What might be good about shopping in this way? What might be bad?**

3 ▶ 10 **Listen to a student talking about food shopping and answer the questions.**

1 How does she prefer shopping, photo A or photo B?
2 Do you agree with her opinions?

Listening
Multiple choice (Part 2)

4 ▶ 11 **You are going to listen to an interview with a woman called Magda on a television technology show.**

1 Look at question 1 in Activity 5 and underline the keywords in the question and options.
2 Listen and answer the question.

6 **Work in pairs and discuss the questions.**

1 Would people in your country like shopping in this kind of virtual supermarket?
2 What do supermarkets in your country do to attract more customers?

A

B

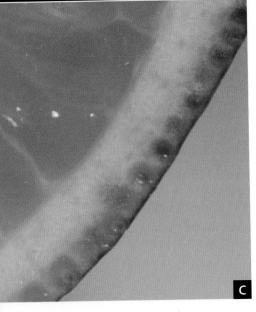

C

Modals of possibility

▶ **GRAMMAR** REFERENCE p.125

1 **Look at picture A. What do you think it is?**

2 ▶ 13 **Listen to the conversation and write the word you hear in the gap.**

1 *It* .... *be* anything like an apple, because they don't have that kind of middle.

2 *It* .... *be* a lemon, they look like that in the centre.

3 *It* .... *be* an orange. It's the right shape for an orange.

3 **Match the modals of possibility from Activity 2 with their meanings A–C.**

A   I'm sure it is.

B   It's possible.

C   I'm sure it's not.

> **LANGUAGE TIP**
>
> *Could, might* and *may* can all be used to say that something is possible in the present or future.

4 **Work in pairs. What do you think the other foods in the photographs are? After you finish discussing, check your answers on page 117.**

5 **Complete the sentences using *must, might/could* or *can't* + a form of the verb *be* or *have*.**

1 The restaurant .... a table tonight if they're not busy.

2 He .... vegetarian because I saw him eating a hotdog.

3 It .... time to go! All the others have left.

4 They .... international food, but I doubt it. It's a local restaurant.

5 This .... past its use-by date. I only bought it this morning.

6 There .... a mistake on this bill. I didn't order champagne!

Speaking

6 **Work in pairs. Turn to page 118 and follow the instructions.**

Speaking

1 **Work in pairs and discuss the questions.**

1 How often do you eat out? What kinds of cafés or restaurants do you go to?

2 What restaurant would you recommend to someone visiting your town/city? Why?

3 Have you ever had a memorable experience at a restaurant? What happened?

Reading

2 **Read the story and answer the questions.**

1 Did the writer have a good or bad experience at the restaurant? Why?

2 Do you think the writer and his friend did the right thing? Why/Why not?

3 What's the purpose of the underlined expressions?

An unexpected treat

When the food arrived, we couldn't believe our eyes. <u>Twenty minutes earlier</u>, we'd ordered soup (the cheapest food on the menu) but here was the waiter with the biggest steaks we'd ever seen!

We knew we should say something, but the food smelt so delicious. We looked at each other and, <u>a moment later</u>, we picked up our forks and ate hungrily.

<u>Eventually</u> the bill came. There was no mention of the steaks so we paid and quickly left the table. <u>Suddenly</u> we heard the waiter shout, 'Excuse me!' We turned around, our hearts beating. 'Don't forget your coats!' he said. We laughed, thanked him and <u>finally</u> walked through the door. <u>Just then</u> we heard two customers asking where their steaks were!

3 **Choose the correct time linker in each sentence. Use the underlined linkers in the story to help you.**

1 We waited for ages before our food *a moment later/ eventually* arrived.

2 The waiter *finally/suddenly* slipped and dropped all the plates.

3 First we had soup, then we had fish. *Finally/Just then* we had cake.

4 I offered to pay the bill. *Just then/Twenty minutes earlier* I realised my wallet was at home.

5 Our waiter was very quick. We ordered the drinks and *a moment later/eventually* they arrived.

6 When the food arrived, it wasn't the dish I'd ordered *suddenly/twenty minutes earlier*.

Writing
Story (Part 3)

▶ **WRITING** REFERENCE p.135

▶ **FUNCTIONS** BANK p.154

EXAM TIP

Use time linkers in your story so your reader can follow the order of events.

4 **Plan and write your answer to the exam task.**

- Your teacher has asked you to write a story.
- This is the title for your story: *A picnic that went wrong*
- Write your **story** in about **100 words**.

PROGRESS TEST 1

1 Put the words in the correct order to make questions. Add an auxiliary verb where necessary.

1 from / you / where / ?
2 name / spell / your / how / you / ?
3 chose / name / who / your / ?
4 studying / you / English / why / ?
5 enjoy / you / sport / doing / ?
6 see / friends / how often / you / your / ?
7 last night / what / do / you / ?
8 your / what / middle / name / ?

2 Match the questions in Activity 1 with the answers A–J.

A I stayed in and watched TV.
B It's Henry, which was my grandad's name.
C I hang out with them once or twice a week.
D My dad.
E Not really. I watch it but I never do any.
F Well, I grew up in Cardiff but I live in London now.
G Because I need to pass an English exam to get into university.
H C-A-R-L-Y.

3 Pilar is at a train station. Rewrite her questions so they are indirect.

1 Where's the ticket office?
Would you mind telling me _____ ?
2 How can I pay for a ticket?
I'd like to know _____ .
3 Does the train leave at 7 p.m.?
Could you tell me _____ ?
4 Has the train left?
Have you any idea _____ ?
5 Can I buy a drink on the train?
Could you tell me _____ ?
6 What time does the train arrive?
Have you any idea _____ ?
7 Is anyone sitting here?
Can you tell me _____ ?
8 Why has the train stopped here?
Do you know _____ ?

4 Complete the text with appropriate words from the list below.

bald   cheerful   curious   curly   good-looking
in her 40s   in his 50s   long   reliable   organised
overweight   sensitive   shy   slim   strange

Hi Phil,

You asked me to email you some photos of my family so here they are! I'll tell you a bit about each person.

My dad's (1) _____ in his 50s now so he's getting old! He used to have blond hair like me but as you can see he's (2) _bald_ these days. He doesn't like speaking to people because he's (3) _shy_ but he's always (4) _cheerful_ so he never stops smiling. My mum's a bit younger than my dad – she's still (5) _in her 40s_ . She's really (6) _organised_ and so plans everything the family does.

My sister's 20 years old. You have to be a bit careful what you say to her because she's quite (7) _sensitive_ . My brother's just turned 13. As you can see, he's a bit (8) _overweight_ because he eats like a horse but I think he's going to be really (9) _good-looking_ and popular with girls when he's older. He never does what he says he's going to do so isn't very (10) _reliable_ though.

Anyway, I'd love to know about your family! Write soon.

Love

Ella

5 Complete the sentences with appropriate words from the list below.

beef   diet   drink   fatty   fish   food   go
local   raw   roast   soft   speciality   stir-fried

1 This fish dish is a _____ _____ in this area.
2 For perfect _____ _____ cover the meat with honey before you put it in the oven.
3 When I lived in Japan, I ate a lot of sushi, which is _____ _____ with rice.
4 Let's have something light like _____ _____ vegetables tonight.
5 Would you like a _____ _____ ? I've got some cola.
6 I eat too much _____ _____ like chips. I need to _____ on a _____ .

6 Read the postcard and choose the correct verb forms.

Place Stamp Here

Post Card

Hi Mum and Dad,

Richie and I **(1)** are having/have a fantastic honeymoon here in the Maldives. Our hotel **(2)** is being/is fantastic and the beaches **(3)** are being/are beautiful. I **(4)** 'm writing/write this postcard in the famous Ithaa restaurant. Ithaa **(5)** is meaning/means 'mother of pearl' in the national language. The restaurant **(6)**'s sitting/sits five metres under the sea, so loads of tourists **(7)** are coming/come here every day to eat and watch the sea life go past. Don't worry, to get down here you **(8)** aren't swimming/don't swim! You **(9)** are walking/walk down some stairs.

Anyway, must go now. The waiter **(10)** 's bringing/brings our food and I **(11)** 'm wanting/want to look at the amazing view. We **(12)** 're looking/look at a baby shark above us right now!

Lots of love,

Kerry xxx

7 Here are some sentences about a new restaurant. Complete the second sentence with modals of possibility so it means the same as the first. Use no more than three words.

1 It's possible that it is a Chinese restaurant because there are dragons painted outside.

There are dragons painted outside, so it could ꞁ be a Chinese restaurant.

2 I'm sure the chef is from China because I heard him speaking Chinese.

The chef must be be from China because I heard him speaking Chinese.

3 It's impossible that the waitress is Chinese – she didn't understand the chef!

The waitress can't be Chinese – she didn't understand the chef!

4 If I go, maybe I'll have to eat with chopsticks.

If I go, I might have to eat with chopsticks.

5 It's impossible that sushi will be on the menu as it's a Japanese dish.

Sushi can't ꞁ be on the menu as it's a Japanese dish.

6 It's certain that people in this town love Chinese food – this is the sixth one on the street!

People in this town must love Chinese food – this is the sixth one on the street!

8 Read the text below and choose the correct word for each space. Choose the correct letter A–C.

Pop-up restaurants

(1) .... you like eating fashionable food in unusual places? Then it's possible you **(2)** .... like pop-up restaurants: temporary restaurants that appear in a place for just a few weeks.

One such restaurant is The Beach Experience in London. **(3)** .... else could you enjoy eating **(4)** .... meat that's been cooked on an open fire on a sandy beach in the middle of London? The idea for the restaurant, which is actually located in a supermarket car park, came from chef . Paul Simpkins.

As a child Paul was a **(5)** .... cook and a big **(6)** .... who spent hours thinking of unusual food ideas. Now, it's clear he's a very **(7)** .... man, wanting to be successful all around the world. Because he grew up on the coast, he's got a strong **(8)** .... to the sea and wants to share his love of the beach with Londoners.

The restaurant has been full since it opened so Paul **(9)** .... be pleased. 'Yes,' he says, touching the **(10)** .... on his chin, 'but it's more important that people enjoy the experience.'

1 A Have   B Are   C Do
2 A might   B must   C did
3 A When   B Where   C Why
4 A raw   B boiled   C barbecued
5 A talented   B better   C shining
6 A imaginer   B inventor   C maker
7 A sensitive   B generous   C ambitious
8 A desire   B partner   C connection
9 A must   B might   C can't
10 A beard   B lip   C tooth

Mind your manners

Speaking

1 Work in pairs. When was the last time someone was rude to you? What happened? How did you feel?

Extended turn (Part 3)

2 Student A, describe the photo at the top of this page. Student B, describe the photo on page 25. Talk for one minute each. Listen and tell your partner if he/she missed any details in the photo.

General conversation (Part 4)

▶ **FUNCTIONS** BANK p.153

3 ▶ 14 You are going to listen to two candidates talking in Part 4 of the Speaking test. Listen and answer the questions.

1 What does the examiner ask them to talk about?
2 Does each candidate speak for a similar amount of time?
3 Do they interact well?

4 Match the phrases the candidates used in Activity 3 to their uses A–E.

1	Sorry, can I say something?	**A**	ask someone to repeat something
2	Sure, go ahead …	**B**	ask someone for their opinion
3	Do you agree?	**C**	tell someone it's okay to speak
4	Sorry, could you say that again?	**D**	check what someone just said
5	I don't get what you mean.	**E**	ask if you can speak
6	You mean (it's really dirty)?	**F**	say you don't understand something

5 Work in pairs. Talk together about things that annoy you. Talk for two or three minutes. Use the expressions in Activity 4 to help you.

EXAM TIP

Summarise what is in the photo and then describe what you can see in more detail. Talk about the place, people and objects.

EXAM TIP

Make sure you both take turns and speak for a similar amount of time in this Part of the exam. You get marks for communicating with each other.

Phrasal verbs

6 **Listen again to what annoys the candidates in Activity 3 and complete sentences 1–10.**

1 …just when I have to .... something important ...... for a piece of work.
2 Usually something I need to .... to my teacher the next day!
3 He loves .... with his friends in his flat.
4 They .... their music ..... so loud that I can't hear my TV.
5 I .... fine with my neighbour but …
6 His owners should .... him more carefully.
7 I usually .... and try again later.
8 Like that's going to .... things ...... !
9 And people who don't .... after their dog in the street!
10 And people who .... talking when other people want to speak.

> **,phrasal 'verb** *n* [C] a verb with an adverb or preposition after it, which has a different meaning from the verb used alone. *Set off*, *look after* and *put up with* are all phrasal verbs.

7 **Match the phrasal verbs in Activity 6 with the meanings A–J.**

A continue
B give something to a boss/teacher
C remove dirt and put things in their correct place
D find information (in a book/on a computer)
E stop trying to do something
F make the volume louder
G have a friendly relationship with
H make somebody/something move more quickly
I be responsible for
J spend time with

8 **Complete the questions with a phrasal verb from Activity 6.**

1 How often do you .... your flat/house?
2 Do you ever .... children? Do you enjoy it?
3 Where do you go to .... the meaning of a new English word?
4 How long do you queue for before you .... and walk away?
5 Who do you .... with the best in your family?
6 Do you usually .... your English homework on time?
7 Who do you .... with at the weekends?
8 When do you .... your music ..... loud?
9 If something is difficult, do you just stop or .... trying?
10 Do people often tell you to .... so you aren't late?

9 **Work in pairs. Take turns to ask and answer five of the questions from Activity 8. Ask each other follow-up questions to get more information.**

Vocabulary

1 **How would you feel in these situations? Choose a word from the list.**

| amused | annoyed | embarrassed |
| excited | satisfied | disgusted |

1 A lasagne that you've cooked tastes pretty good.
2 Your friend has made you a cake in the shape of hamburger.
3 You've won a free meal at the best restaurant in town.
4 A salesperson has phoned during your favourite TV programme.
5 You've fallen off your chair at a party.
6 You find an insect in your meal.

2 **When did you last feel amused, annoyed, disgusted, embarassed, excited or satisfied?**

EXAM TIP

You might have to understand a person's attitude, as well as factual information. Listen for words that give clues about attitude.

Listening
True/False (Part 4)

3 **Look at the notice below. Would you like to try this kind of club?**

THE SUPPER CLUB

Would you like to make new friends? Are you tired of cooking meals for one? Join the Wessex University Supper Club! We'll match you up with a group of four or five other students.

You'll take turns to cook for each other and provide a little entertainment after the meal. It's a great chance to make new friends and try new things. If you're a bit shy, don't worry: sign up with a friend!

Text Dan on 0789 463291 for more details.

The Supper Club

4 **You will hear a boy called Steve and a girl called Becky, talking about their evening at the University Supper Club. Before you listen, read sentences 1–6 and underline the keywords.**

		A	B
1	Becky was excited about trying the new supper club.	☐	☐
2	Steve was confident that the others would like his cooking.	☐	☐
3	They were both annoyed by the other girl in the group.	☐	☐
4	Becky was surprised by the entertainment.	☐	☐
5	Steve disliked the other boy at the dinner.	☐	☐
6	They both agree the next meal will be better.	☐	☐

5 ▶ **15 Listen and decide if the sentences in Activity 4 are correct. If it is correct, put a tick (✓) in the box under A for YES. If it is not correct, put a tick (✓) under B for NO.**

Speaking

6 **Work in pairs and discuss the questions.**

1 Have you ever been in a social situation when you didn't know many people? What was it like?
2 What meal could you cook at a Supper Club dinner? What entertainment would you arrange?

-ing and infinitives

▶ **GRAMMAR** REFERENCE p.125

1 **Work in pairs and discuss the questions.**

1 What do you think is the best way to meet new people?

2 What do you think makes a good friend?

2 ▶ **16** **Listen to some people giving their opinions on friendship for a radio show. Do you agree with what they say?**

3 **Listen again and complete the sentences with the word or words you hear.**

1 Someone who'll watch the football without .... !

2 .... your friend will help you.

3 Someone you enjoy .... time with.

4 It's important .... near each other.

5 Someone you can't wait .... your news with.

4 **Look at the sentences in Activity 3 and complete the rules with either -ing form or infinitive. Use the:**

1 .... after some verbs such as *mind, enjoy, keep.*

2 .... after some verbs such as *expect, learn, can't wait.*

3 .... when the verb is the subject or object of a sentence.

4 .... after a preposition (*after, on, before, etc.*).

5 .... after an adjective (*pleased, happy, etc.*).

LANGUAGE TIP

Some verbs can be followed by both the -*ing* form and the infinitive but the meaning is the same, e.g. *start, begin, continue, prefer.* I started **laughing**. / I started **to laugh**.

5 **Read the blog about kindness. Choose the best words 1–5.**

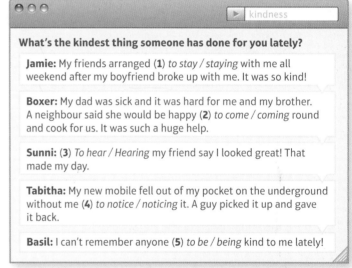

What's the kindest thing someone has done for you lately?

Jamie: My friends arranged (**1**) *to stay / staying* with me all weekend after my boyfriend broke up with me. It was so kind!

Boxer: My dad was sick and it was hard for me and my brother. A neighbour said she would be happy (**2**) *to come / coming* round and cook for us. It was such a huge help.

Sunni: (**3**) *To hear / Hearing* my friend say I looked great! That made my day.

Tabitha: My new mobile fell out of my pocket on the underground without me (**4**) *to notice / noticing* it. A guy picked it up and gave it back.

Basil: I can't remember anyone (**5**) *to be / being* kind to me lately!

Speaking

6 **Work in pairs and discuss the questions.**

1 What's the kindest thing someone has done for you recently?

2 What's the kindest thing you've done for somebody else recently?

7 **You have decided to sign up to a social networking site. Turn to page 118 and complete the questionnaire.**

8 **Work in small groups. Ask questions about their answers to Activity 7. Can you find someone with similar interests?**

Speaking

1 **Work in pairs and discuss the questions.**

1 What do you use your mobile phone for? Do you ever use it to learn English?

2 How often do you check your text messages or surf the internet?

3 How often do you change your ringtone?

4 What are good and bad mobile phone manners?

Reading

True/False (Part 3)

2 **Look at the article title and headings. What do you think it's about? Read the article quickly and check.**

3 **Look at the sentences about mobile phone manners and underline the keywords.**

		A	B
1	Research shows people know they have bad mobile phone manners in public.	✓	☐
2	Putting your phone on silent might surprise your friends.	✓	☐
3	It is a good idea to use different ringtones in different locations.	☐	✓
4	Using a mobile while driving is permitted under certain conditions.	✓	☐
5	It is acceptable to use your mobile in certain parts of a train.	✓	☐
6	If the signal breaks down, you should wait for the person to call you back.	☐	✓
7	You should warn people in advance if you are going to take an important call.	✓	☐
8	It's a good idea to keep your mobile where you can see it during a meal.	☐	✓
9	You can save time by making calls while doing other business.	☐	✓
10	Debrett's have already published a number of guides on good manners.	✓	☐

EXAM TIP

Underline the keywords in the sentences to help you find the information in the text. The sentences are in the same order as the text, so always start with question 1.

4 **Read the text to decide if each sentence is correct (A) or incorrect (B).**

Vocabulary

Phrasal verbs

5 **Complete the questions with the bold phrasal verbs in the article.**

1 You miss a friend's call. Do you call them or wait for them to .... you .... ?

2 Do you often .... people .... while you're in a public place? Where?

3 Do you .... your mobile .... as soon as you wake up? Why/Why not?

4 Do you .... your mobile phone .... before your lesson starts? Why/Why not?

5 You're speaking to a friend when your mobile rings. Do you .... talking to your friend or answer the phone? Why/Why not?

6 You're talking on your phone in a shop queue. Do you .... and put the phone away when you get to the front? Why/Why not?

6 **Work in pairs. Take turns to ask and answer the questions in Activity 5.**

Speaking

7 **Work in groups and discuss the questions.**

1 Do we need to be told how to behave in social situations? Why/Why not?

2 In which situations do you think people need more information on how to behave politely? Why?

_____

on the internet   using public transport

in the street   on holiday   in a restaurant

_____

8 **In your groups, choose one of the situations and write a set of eight rules telling people what good manners are. Present your ideas to the class.**

Mobile manners

Do you find the use of mobile phones in public places hugely annoying? Then you're not alone.

According to new research, it annoys people all over the world, and yet more of us are doing it. Most people interviewed said other people's manners were terrible, while their own manners were good, but they still continue to use their phones in public without thinking about the effect on others. Here are some rules to help you use your mobile phone more responsibly in public places.

Keep the noise down

You know your phone is too loud when it screams out and people turn to look at you. Remember the *silent* function. Your friends might not expect to see you suddenly dive into your bag to answer a vibrating phone, but they'll be grateful they won't have to listen to your new ringtone.

On the subject of ringtones: if you're embarrassed by your phone when it rings (e.g. on trains, in offices, or when you're visiting your mother), you've almost certainly made the wrong choice of ringtone. Choose one you can use anywhere.

Think of others

Make sure that your phone conversation is not disturbing other people. Private conversations are never good in front of others – be respectful. Never **ring up** a friend in public and have a huge argument, or use bad language or talk about money.

Location, location

Switch off your phone when you are going into meetings, cinemas and so on. Only make or take calls in the car with legal hands-free equipment or you face getting a rather large fine.

Don't use your phone in 'quiet zones' on trains (those areas where electronic equipment must be kept on silent). When the signal is bad, explain to the caller that there's a problem and **hang up**. Don't shout 'Hello?!' loudly several times if you lose the connection. **Call** the other person **back** as soon as you can, even if it's only to say goodbye.

Remember me?

The people you're with deserve more attention than your mobile. If you're in a meeting or with friends, don't **turn** your phone **on** unless you are waiting for an important call that you must take. In that situation, don't wait until it rings. Explain at the very beginning that you're expecting to take a call.

There's nothing quite as bad as having a mobile phone conversation or texting at the dinner table. Don't even put your phone on the table or look at it mid-conversation. And don't **carry on** mobile phone calls while you are being served in banks, shops and so on. It's impolite not to give people who are working there your full attention.

The well-known publishing company Debrett's, which has been publishing guides on how to behave in British society for the last 60 years, can offer further advice on mobile phone use. Go to their website for more details about using your phone politely.

Reading

1 Work in pairs and discuss the questions.

1 What kind of things do families argue about?
2 Do younger people have the same manners as older people? How are they different?

2 Read the email and answer the questions.

1 What's the relationship between Josie, Tommy and Stephanie?
2 Why is Stephanie annoyed?

3 Work in pairs and discuss the questions.

1 Who do you feel most sorry for?
2 What advice would you give to these people?

▶ Search

| ADVICE | RESPOND | NEWS |

MOTHER-IN-LAW SENDS ANGRY EMAIL

Getting along with your future parents-in-law can be difficult, and Josie Carlton is facing a greater challenge than most. Her fiancé's mother has sent her an angry email that is quickly becoming a huge internet hit.

Dear Miss Carlton,

As you're going to join our family, I feel I ¹*must* write to you about your manners. After all, you ²*have to* respect the house rules when you're in another home. You ³*shouldn't* announce what you will and won't eat unless you're allergic to something. You ⁴*mustn't* start your meal before everyone else. You ⁵*should* get up instead of lying in bed until late morning when everyone else rises early.

I understand your parents can't help pay for the wedding. Of course, they ⁶*don't have to* save for their daughter's wedding, but tradition does expect it. I suggest you change your plans and have a smaller wedding, which you can afford.

I'm sure you feel very fortunate to be marrying my son. I only hope Tommy doesn't regret his decision.

Stephanie Smythe

Modals of obligation

▶ **GRAMMAR** REFERENCE p.126

4 Match the examples of modals of obligation 1–6 in the text in Activity 2 with the rules A–E. There are two examples for one of the rules.

A personal/internal obligation
B external obligation
C no obligation
D prohibition
E used to give advice

LANGUAGE TIP

You can also use *make/let someone do something* to express obligation and permission.
My dad **made me get a job** during the school holidays.
My aunt **lets me sleep in** late when I visit.

5 Complete the blog comments with the modals of obligation from Activity 2.

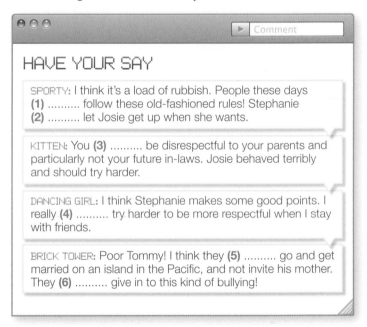

HAVE YOUR SAY

SPORTY: I think it's a load of rubbish. People these days **(1)** .... follow these old-fashioned rules! Stephanie **(2)** .... let Josie get up when she wants.

KITTEN: You **(3)** .... be disrespectful to your parents and particularly not your future in-laws. Josie behaved terribly and should try harder.

DANCING GIRL: I think Stephanie makes some good points. I really **(4)** .... try harder to be more respectful when I stay with friends.

BRICK TOWER: Poor Tommy! I think they **(5)** .... go and get married on an island in the Pacific, and not invite his mother. They **(6)** .... give in to this kind of bullying!

Speaking

6 Work in pairs and discuss the questions.

1 Are there any social rules like this in your country?
2 What advice would you give someone who wanted to marry into your family?

Speaking

1 **Work in pairs and discuss the questions.**

1 Have you ever heard of themed weddings? What are they?

2 What do you think a *Star Wars* themed wedding would be like?

3 What theme would you choose for your wedding?

Writing

Message (Part 2)

▶ **WRITING** REFERENCE p.149

▶ **FUNCTIONS** BANK p.154

2 **Read the emails that two friends have sent to you.**

1 Why are they writing?

2 Which email is better, Sandy's or Josh's? Why?

Web mail

Dear Sophie
I see that you're engaged. I won't be at the engagement party next week. I might see you another time.
Sandy

Web mail

Dear Sophie
You're getting married? Congratulations! **(1)** Thanks for inviting me to your engagement party, but **(2)** I'm afraid I can't come because I'm away on business.
(3) Shall we get together next month? **(4)** I'll cook for you and Dave. **(5)** I definitely want to celebrate with you both. Have fun!
Josh

---

3 **Look at the two emails again. Match the underlined phrases to their functions.**

apologising 2   offering 4   showing interest 5
suggesting 3   thanking 1

> **EXAM TIP**
>
> Make your email friendly and clear by using some functional phrases.

4 **Read the exam task below and answer the questions.**

1 Who will you write to?

2 What information will you include?

3 What functional phrases will you include?

4 How many words will you write?

> Your friend Hannah is having a *Star Wars* themed wedding next month. You are invited. Now you are writing to her about the party. Write to Hannah and
> * accept the invitation
> * ask what you should wear
> * suggest something you can help with
> Write an **email** of **35–45 words**.

5 **Write your email.**

6 **Pass the email to a partner to check that you have included the points below. Rewrite your email if you have forgotten any of these.**

1 all three content points   3 enough words

2 enough functional phrases   4 complete sentences

4

Speaking

1 **Work in pairs and discuss the questions.**

1. Are there any historical places or buildings in your city/town? Describe them.
2. What's the most interesting historical place or building you've visited? Why?
3. Which historical place or building would you like to visit in the world? Why?

Reading

Multiple-choice cloze (Part 5)

EXAM TIP

Look at each gap carefully and think about what word is missing before you read the four options and choose the best one.

2 **Read the headline of the text below. What do you think the text is about? Read the text quickly to see if you are correct.**

3 **Read the text more carefully. What word do you think goes in each gap? Compare your ideas in pairs.**

TheDailyNews

New technology finds old history

History professor David Kennedy has **(0)** _C discovered_ almost 2,000 ancient sites in Saudi Arabia, **despite** being in Australia. **(1)** ..C.... of using traditional tools, he found the underground sites from space using satellite technology **(2)** ..B..... to everyone.

To find the sites, David looked at hundreds of images **and (3)** ..A.... them to pictures of known sites. **As well as that**, he asked a friend **(4)** ..D..... lives in Saudi to visit two locations and take photos. These **(5)** ..D.... his results. The professor believes the sites could be **(6)** ..B..... 8,000 years old, **although** he cannot be sure without tests on the ground.

Traditionally, this kind of technology was expensive and only available to scientists. **However**, these days an internet connection is enough, and ordinary people can **also** get involved. In fact, thousands of people have **(7)** ..D..... in the search since satellite images of Earth **(8)** ..B...... online, so we can **(9)** B....... more discoveries like this **(10)** ..C.... the future.

4 **Look at the example (0). Then choose the best option for each gap 1–10 from the four choices.**

0	**A** collected	**B** got	**C** **discovered**	**D** realised
1	**A** Rather	**B** Enough	**C** Instead	**D** Even
2	**A** possible	**B** available	**C** spare	**D** public
3	**A** compared	**B** measured	**C** studied	**D** checked
4	**A** where	**B** which	**C** whose	**D** who
5	**A** approved	**B** decided	**C** agreed	**D** confirmed
6	**A** more	**B** over	**C** close	**D** near
7	**A** shared	**B** interested	**C** involved	**D** joined
8	**A** showed	**B** appeared	**C** displayed	**D** arranged
9	**A** look	**B** expect	**C** suppose	**D** wait
10	**A** at	**B** on	**C** in	**D** for

Speaking

5 **Work in pairs and discuss the questions.**

1 Which other parts of the world might have hidden sites like this? What would you expect to find there?

2 What are the advantages and disadvantages of this kind of technology?

Vocabulary

Linking words: addition and contrast

6 **Look at the linking words in bold in the text. Work in pairs and answer the questions.**

1 Which add information?

2 Which show contrast?

3 Which join two clauses?

4 Which start a new sentence?

5 Which is followed by an *-ing* form?

7 **Rewrite the ideas using the linking words in brackets.**

1 I'm interested in history. I don't have time to watch many programmes about it. (*despite*)

2 I'd love to discover something with satellite technology. I don't really have time. (*however*)

3 I love going to busy cities. I enjoy visiting historical sites. (*as well as that*)

4 I hope to see the Egyptian pyramids one day. It's not cheap to get there. (*although*)

5 I read a lot of books about the world. I learn a lot from the internet. (*also*)

6 There's a famous historical site in my country. I haven't been there. (*though*)

7 I studied history at school. I haven't looked at a history book for years. (*in spite of*)

8 **Work in pairs. Which of the sentences in Activity 7 are true for you? Can you change any of the other sentences so they are true for you?**

Speaking

1 Work in pairs. Have you ever been involved in a project, for example a sports project, arts project, community project or project at work or school? What was it? Did you enjoy it?

Reading

2 Read the article. Would you be interested in working on this project? Why/Why not?

NEWS

Last updated at 08:38

Video & Audio | Magazine | Editor's Blog | In Pictures

It's all Greek to me

The Egypt Exploration Society and the University of Oxford **(1)** *have put* thousands of pieces of valuable documents, all written in ancient Greek, online as part of a project called *Ancient Lives*. They want people at home to help them translate them. The texts were written almost 2,000 years ago when Egypt was under the control of Greece. Two students **(2)** *discovered* them in 1896 buried under sand in an ancient rubbish dump. It took them ten years to collect almost 200,000 pieces. *Since* that time, the university **(3)** *has looked after* the documents, which include literature and letters that tell us about life 2,000 years ago.

Students **(4)** *have studied* the texts *for* decades but they **(5)** *haven't translated* them all yet. In fact, they've examined just two percent. The University of Oxford says you shouldn't worry if you've never studied Greek. You just need to match the characters the computer shows you. So anyone can have a go.

Present perfect and past simple

▶ **GRAMMAR** REFERENCE p.126

3 Match verbs 1–5 in the text with the uses of the past simple and present perfect A–D. You will need to use one rule twice.

We use the

A **past simple** to talk about an action that started and finished in the past. We are talking about a specific past time.

B **present perfect** to talk about an action that started and finished in the past but the time is unknown, unimportant or very recent.

C **present perfect** with *for/since* to talk about an action that started in the past and is continuing now.

D **present perfect** with *ever, never, already, yet* and *just*.

LANGUAGE TIP

We use *for* when we describe the length of an action. We use *since* when we describe the starting point of an action. *I've lived in London **for** two years. I've worked here **since** 2009.*

4 Which time expressions are used with *for* and which with *since*?

yesterday	three hours	a few days
this morning	my birthday	two minutes
last year	February	a long time
a week	I was a child	months

5 Work in pairs. What is the difference in meaning between these two sentences?

1 They were in Egypt for ten years.
2 They've been in Egypt for ten years.

6 Work in pairs. Use the prompts in 1–6. Take turns to ask and answer questions starting with *How long*.

1 be/a student here?
2 know/closest friend?
3 live/in your house?
4 have/your hairstyle?
5 own/your mobile?
6 like/your favourite musician or band?

7 Turn to page 118. Follow the instructions.

Speaking
Simulated situation (Part 2)

▶ **FUNCTIONS** BANK p.153

1 Work in pairs and discuss the questions.

1 Do you have a special object at home that you could never throw out? Why is it so special? Where do you keep it?

2 Why do people keep objects that aren't useful?

2 Look at the list of objects below. Work in small groups. Have you ever kept any of these objects at home? Talk about each object.

a concert programme   a soft toy   a T-shirt
a sports ticket   a photograph

3 ▶ 17 Listen to two people deciding which of the objects in Activity 2 to take to the 'Bring-a-thing-a-thon'. What objects do they decide to take?

4 Listen again and complete the sentences with the phrase you hear.

1 .... go for the most valuable?

2 They should have a special memory for the owner. .... ?

3 .... taking a photo?

4 .... take your concert programme.

EXAM TIP

Use the language of suggestions while you talk, and summarise your choice and reasons at the end.

5 Do the exam task below.

Your town is holding an exhibition called *Inventions we can't live without*, and the organisers want you to help them choose objects for the exhibition. Talk together about how each object is useful in everyday life and decide which is the most useful.

6 Assess your performance.

1 Did you speak about all the objects in the picture? If not, which did you miss?

2 Did you use the language of suggestions? If not, which phrases could you use?

3 Did you clearly summarise your decision at the end?

Speaking

1 **Work in pairs and discuss the questions.**

1 How often do you go to museums and art galleries? Do you enjoy going to them? Why/Why not?

2 Which do you think is the best museum in your country? Why?

3 What do you think makes a good museum?

Listening

Multiple choice (Part 1)

2 **You are going to complete Part 1 of the Listening test. Before you listen, work in pairs and look at question 1. What language do you expect to hear?**

> **EXAM TIP**
>
> In Listening Part 1, study the pictures quickly and identify the main differences before you start to listen to the recording.

3 ▶ 18 **Listen to the recording. For each question, choose the correct picture.**

1 Where is the museum?

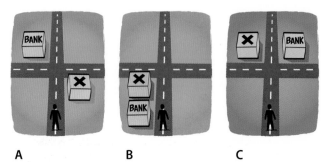

A   B   C

2 Which object did the students find part of?

A   B   C

3 How was the picture damaged in the fire?

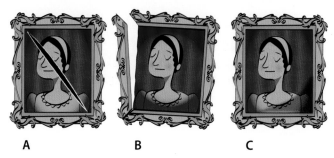

A   B   C

4 What does the girl buy?

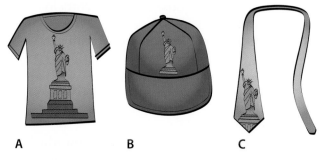

A   B   C

5 What will the weather be like during the fair?

A   B   C

6 Which animal is on the plate?

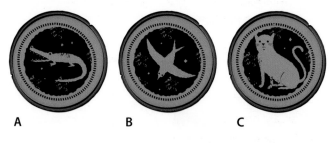

A   B   C

7 When can students visit the show for free?

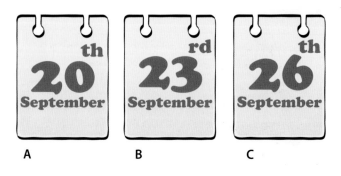

A   B   C

Speaking

1 **Work in pairs and discuss the questions.**

1 What personal records of your past do you have?

2 Describe one of your old school photographs.

Listening

2 ▶ 19 **You will hear a man describing one of the old school photos on this page. Which photo is he describing?**

used to

▶ **GRAMMAR** REFERENCE p.126

3 **Listen again and tick (✓) the box to say whether each description was in the past or now.**

		Past	Now
1	have brown hair	☐	☐
2	have blonde hair	☐	☐
3	wear normal clothes	☐	☐
4	be a leader of fashion	☐	☐
5	look sweet	☐	☐
6	be called Stefani	☐	☐

4 **Look at sentences A and B and choose the correct words to complete the rule.**

used to refers to things that *were true in the past / are true in the present.*

A She *used to have* long, brown hair and a very normal kind of haircut.

B She *used to wear* normal clothes, really.

LANGUAGE TIP

to is pronounced in its weak form, /tə/

5 **Complete the sentences with the correct form of *used to* and an appropriate verb.**

1 The girl in Picture A .... short hair back then.

2 The girl in Picture A .... a really lovely smile.

3 The girl in Picture B .... really sweet.

4 Did the girl in Picture B .... earrings? I can't really see.

5 The boy in Picture C .... glasses, but I'm sure he does now.

6 I don't think the boy in Picture D .... a very good haircut.

Speaking

6 **The four photos A–D show famous people when they were at school. Who do you think they could be? Check your ideas with the more recent photos on page 118.**

7 **Work in pairs and describe how the people in the photographs used to look before they were famous. How have they changed?**

8 **What did you use to look like six years ago? Tell your partner.**

Speaking

1 The photos show Shanghai in the 1920s and today. Work in pairs and discuss.

1 How has Shanghai changed?

2 What has stayed the same?

Listening

2 ▶ **20 You will hear a radio interview with a British woman talking about life in Shanghai. Listen and decide if each sentence is correct (A) or incorrect (B).**

1 Shanghai has the fastest *population growth* in China.

2 Shanghai has poor *public transport*.

3 People are concerned about the lack of *fresh air*.

4 *Open spaces* can be found all around the city.

5 There are *playgrounds* for kids in every park.

6 There are good *entertainment facilities* in Shanghai.

7 Shanghai has a *mild climate*.

8 Shanghai offers good *work opportunities*.

3 Work in pairs and discuss the questions.

1 What sounds attractive about living in Shanghai?

2 What would make it difficult to live in Shanghai?

Town and city

4 How are the words in *italics* in Activity 2 created, a) noun + noun or b) adjective + noun?

> **LANGUAGE TIP**
>
> Compound nouns are two or more words that are used together as a noun (e.g. *ice cream*).
>
> Collocations are words which are often used together (e.g. *mild climate*, not ~~weak~~ *climate*; *have a cup of tea*, not ~~take~~ *a cup of tea*).

5 Which of the nouns in the box collocate with a) *fresh*; b) *public*; c) *work*?

bread	book	experience	fruit
holiday	ideas	man	opinion
out	services	start	toilets

6 ▶ **21 You will hear three people describing where they live. Listen and match the Speakers 1–3 to the places where they live A–C.**

A the city   **B** the suburbs   **C** the countryside

7 Match sentence beginnings 1–6 with endings A–F. Then listen again to check your answers.

1 There isn't a *lot*   **A** *from anywhere.*

2 There aren't any *local*   **B** *neighbours.*

3 I have *friendly*   **C** *rents where I live.*

4 My family lives *miles*   **D** *going on where I live.*

5 There are really *high*   **E** *shops near my house.*

6 I live in a *lively*   **F** *neighbourhood.*

Speaking

8 Work in pairs. Are the sentences in Activity 7 true for you? Why/Why not?

9 Which do you think is better, living in the country, the suburbs or the city? Use the ideas below to help you.

distance you travel every day

method of travel   size of home   lifestyle

effect on the environment   shopping

Speaking

1 Work in pairs and discuss the questions.

1 How is information about your country's population collected?

2 Has this changed over the last hundred years?

3 What kind of information is collected?

Writing

Sentence transformations (Part 1)

2 Look at the example sentences in Activity 3, about population records. Do they mean the same thing or different things? What language do you think is being tested in these sentences?

EXAM TIP

Read both sentences and think about what language is being tested before you complete the second sentence. This will help you to choose the right words.

3 These sentences are about population records. Complete the second sentence so it means the same as the first. Use no more than three words.

0 *The first population information was collected 5,000 years ago.*
   Countries __have collected__ population information for 5,000 years.

1 The Chinese government owns the oldest population records in the world.
   The oldest population records in the world _belong_ to the Chinese government.

2 It is expensive to collect population information.
   Collecting population information is expensive.

3 The US government started keeping population records in 1790.
   The US government _have kept_ population records since 1790.

4 It's necessary for adults to give information about themselves and their family.
   Adults _have to give_ information about themselves and their family.

5 No information about individual people is shown to the public.
   The public isn't shown _any information_ about individual people.

4 Look at your answers to Activity 3. Match them with the kind of language (A–E) that is being tested.

A modals of obligation

B word meaning and use

C present perfect/past simple

D negatives

E the -ing form

Speaking

5 Work in pairs and discuss the questions.

1 What do you think are the advantages of keeping population records?

2 Do you think that too much information about us is recorded? Why/Why not? How will this change in future?

NAMES of each Person who abode therein on the Night of Sunday, June 6th.	Age of Males.	Age of Females.	OCCU
The Queen		20	✓
H.R.H. Prince Albert	20		✓
The Princess Royal		6 months	✓
Earl of Aboyne	45		Lord
George Thos Keppel	40		Groom
Edward Praetorius	30		Secretary to
Thomas Batchelor	55		Page of
Augustus Fredk Gerding	40		Page of
William Peel	30		Page of th
George Wakeley	50		Queen's
Thomas Hill	40		Queen
Isaac Carl	30		Val
Andrew Dehler	30		Valett H.
Thomas Cooper	25		Vale
Charles Woolger	30		Vale
James Woods	30		Vale

Name of the Institution _Buckingham_

PROGRESS TEST 2

1 Here are some sentences about keeping an online journal. Complete the second sentence so that it means the same as the first. Use no more than three words.

1 Many people find writing online journals more exciting than paper journals.

People are more .... about writing online journals than paper journals.

2 You can use your online journal to find information years later.

You can use your online journal to .... up information years later.

3 It doesn't matter if you stop writing for a few weeks.

It doesn't matter if you .... up writing for a few weeks.

4 It's important to continue writing every year though.

It's important to .... on writing every year though.

5 Things which embarrass you will not appear publically.

No .... things will appear publically.

6 You'll feel very satisfied when you look back over your work.

Looking back over your work gives you a very .... feeling.

2 Read the extract from a website and choose the correct form of the verb (*to* infinitive or the *-ing* form) to complete the sentences.

The key to success – Think of others! ▶

It may seem obvious, but **(1)** *to be / being* able to get along with others affects how successful you are in life. Other people are always pleased **(2)** *to meet / meeting* cheerful, thoughtful individuals. It's important to learn **(3)** *to forgive / forgiving* others for their mistakes. **(4)** *To hold / Holding* on to bad memories will always make it harder **(5)** *to form / forming* new friendships or **(6)** *to build / building* on the relationships you already have and that will stop you from **(7)** *move / moving* forwards. The best thing about **(8)** *to make / making* other people feel good is that you can expect **(9)** *to feel / feeling* better yourself when you help people. Next time you're having a bad day, cheer yourself up just by **(10)** *to show / showing* a little extra kindness.

---

3 Complete the sentences 1–8 about manners with the correct phrase (*have to / don't have to / mustn't*).

> **Things I've learnt on my travels!**
>
> **1** In the USA, you .... arrive on time. It's really bad if you're late.
>
> **2** In Canada, you .... eat with your knife and fork all the time. Some foods are fine to pick up in your fingers.
>
> **3** In Norway, you .... address people as Mr or Mrs they'll think it really strange.
>
> **4** In Australia, you .... worry too much about manners, just say please and thank you and that's enough.
>
> **5** In South Africa, you .... learn how to use a knife and fork properly. 'Digging' with your fork is considered really bad.
>
> **6** In Germany, you .... bring wine when you are invited to someone's house for dinner, but if you do, make sure it's imported wine, not German wine.
>
> **7** In China, you .... be really careful how you use your chopsticks. You can't stir food with them, point them at someone, lick them or stand them up on your food.
>
> **8** In Argentina, you .... eat walking down the street. Either wait until you're home, or find a café.

4 Combine the two sentences using the word in CAPITALS.

1 Autobiographies are personal stories. Some things appear in all of them.   HOWEVER

2 There's always a chapter on the terrible teacher who hated me. There's usually a chapter on the first girlfriend or boyfriend.   ALSO

3 Some people try to write honestly. Most people use their autobiography to make themselves look good.   ALTHOUGH

4 Celebrity autobiographies sell well. They get bad reviews.   DESPITE

5 An important politician can earn over £1 million before anyone buys the book. They can make another half a million selling the autobiography to newspapers.   AS WELL AS THAT

6 Autobiographies about difficult childhoods sell well. They are not always true.   IN SPITE OF

5 **Match the first half of the sentences 1–8 with the second half A–H.**

1 I've never been
2 I phoned my boyfriend
3 I played for
4 I've already seen
5 I went to a really great show
6 I gave my friend
7 I haven't played
8 I've seen the film *Twilight*

A Lady Gaga in concert five times!
B with my dad last week.
C the school team last year.
D at least 50 times since it came out on DVD.
E to a really formal party before in my life.
F some flowers for her birthday at the weekend.
G tennis since I was at school.
H every day when I was on holiday.

6 **Complete the sentences about finding your family history with a positive or negative form of *used to*.**

1 In the past, only wealthy families .... know about their family history.
2 Learning about a family's past .... be easy in the days before the internet.
3 Religious organisations .... keep records of births, marriages and deaths.
4 Newspapers might contain information as many families .... advertise important family events.
5 Most places of work .... keep any personal details, only the technical information, like their job.
6 If you're lucky enough to have one family member who .... keep a diary, you can read about their hopes and dreams.

7 **Look at the passage below and choose the correct word A–D to complete the gaps.**

SCHOOL • ISSUE 26

How to find new friends

School and university are wonderful places to make new friends, but after you leave, finding new friends isn't as easy as it **(1)** .... to be. There are still ways to add to your collection of friends.

Start talking
You'll need to **(2)** .... yourself start somewhere, so start small, chatting to shop assistants, for example. It'll help you to become a more open person.

Go out
(3) .... you might not be the nightclub type, you need to go out. You can't **(4)** .... to make new friends from the sofa, and nobody's going to be able to **(5)** .... you up without your number. It can be a good idea to **(6)** .... places on the internet where you'll feel comfortable.

Keep an open mind
Don't **(7)** .... just because someone's shy at the beginning. You're looking for kindness and support, not perfection.

Take control
If someone you've **(8)** .... met seems promising, you **(9)** .... be the person to end the conversation. Just say something like, 'I have to go, but I'd love to hang out another time'. It ends things positively, and the other person will probably be **(10)** .... forward to seeing you again soon.

	A	B	C	D
1	could	had	was	used
2	let	do	allow	make
3	In spite of	Despite	Although	However
4	practise	enjoy	refuse	expect
5	ring	hang	hurry	speak
6	turn up	find out	look up	carry on
7	look after	give up	get along	hand in
8	never	yet	just	for
9	should	mustn't	don't have to	need
10	looking	hoping	waiting	seeing

5/10

Swap it

Speaking

1 Work in pairs and look at the photo. Would you like to swap your clothes for catwalk clothes? Why/Why not?

Listening

2 ▶ 22 You will hear a conversation between Will and his sister Jess. Listen and answer the questions.

1 What offer did Will receive this morning?

2 Why does his sister think it's funny?

3 Match the first half of the sentences 1–7 with the second half A–G. Listen again to check.

1 Will's sister thinks he *put* his clothes *on*	**A** *worn out*.
2 Will's shirt doesn't	**B** in the dark this morning.
3 Most of Will's jeans are	**C** *irons* his *clothes*.
4 Will doesn't like	**D** *trying on* clothes.
5 Will often buys clothes that	**E** don't *fit*.
6 Will's mum	**F** *go with* his jeans.

4 Work in pairs. Do you think Will should accept the offer? Why/Why not?

Verbs related to clothes

5 Complete the questions with the words in *italics* in Activity 3.

1 Does it take you long to decide what clothes to .... in the morning?

2 Do you try to choose shoes that .... well .... your clothes?

3 Do you own a pair of .... jeans with holes in them?

4 Do you .... clothes .... before you buy them?

5 Do you .... your .... after you've washed them?

6 How often do you buy clothes that don't .... you?

6 Work in pairs. Take turns to ask and answer the questions in Activity 5.

Order of adjectives

7 Look at Jess's description of Will as a catwalk model and complete the rule with the words below.

material	~~opinion~~
colour	size

'Today, ladies and gentleman, our model is wearing a *beautiful long red leather* coat, green trousers and a lovely purple manbag.'

When we use more than one adjective to describe something, we put the adjectives in this order: opinion, ... , ... , ...

8 Put the adjectives in the correct order in the sentences.

1 Mike's bought a (*green/silk/lovely*) tie.
2 Can I borrow your (*cotton/long*) jacket?
3 Look at that (*red/awful/woollen*) jumper!
4 I'd like those (*big/fantastic/white*) trainers!
5 Hanna's wearing a (*tight/yellow/horrible*) tracksuit.
6 I like this (*leather/black/small*) laptop bag.

9 ▶ 23 Listen to the sentences and mark the intonation. The first one has been done for you.

1 *Mike's bought a lovely, green, silk tie.*

10 Work in pairs and go to page 120.

Speaking

Extended turn (Part 3)

11 ▶ 24 Work in pairs. Listen to a candidate describing the photo on page 42 and answer the questions.

1 How long does she speak for?
2 What else could she describe?

12 Student A, describe photo A for one minute. Student B, describe photo B for one minute. Does your partner use adjectives?

General conversation (Part 4)

13 Work in pairs. The photos in Activity 12 showed people swapping clothes. Now talk together about clothes for three to four minutes. Here are some things you could talk about.

1 The kinds of clothes you usually wear and whether fashion is important to you.
2 How your taste in clothes has changed over the last few years.
3 Which clothes are fashionable among young people at the moment.
4 How young people dress differently to their parents or grandparents.

EXAM TIP

Don't forget to ask questions to find out if your partner has the same opinions as you.

Listening
Gap-fill (Part 3)

1 **Work in pairs and discuss the questions.**

1 Do you drive a car? Why/Why not?

2 What can you tell about a person from the car they drive?

3 Would you use a car rental company rather than own a car? Why/Why not?

2 **You will hear a woman talking about a new way of sharing rented cars among neighbours. Before you listen, read the text and predict the kinds of words that might complete the gaps.**

3 ▶ **25** **Listen and complete each gap with one word from the recording.**

4 **Work in pairs and discuss the questions.**

1 Is it easy for young people to own and drive a car in your country? Why/Why not?

2 Would you be happy to use a scheme like the Valley University car share scheme? Why/Why not?

EXAM TIP

When you predict the information in the gaps, you might not guess the correct answer, but doing this will help you to concentrate.

VU **VALLEY**
UNIVERSITY

Valley Cars: car share scheme

Who can join the scheme?

■ You must be more than **(1)** .... years old to apply.

How does it work?

■ Members will receive a **(2)** '.......................' card when they join.

■ Booking a car by **(3)** .... is the best option.

■ Cars are kept in **(4)** .... Avenue.

How do I apply?

■ Annual membership costs **(5)** ....

■ There's also an application fee and daily charges.

■ During the **(6)** .... , charges are higher.

Reading

1 **Read the text about the Valley University car share scheme and answer the questions.**

1 What do you think the purpose of the text is?

2 What were some of the benefits of using the car scheme?

Don't listen to what we say about Valley Cars, listen to our customers!

'Insuring a car at my age is so expensive. The Valley Cars scheme was **(1)** *cheaper* than running my own car.'

'Booking was **(2)** *easier* than I'd expected. A quick text and I got myself a car!'

'Using Valley Cars **(3)** *was as easy as* borrowing my mum's car!'

'It was **(4)** *more convenient* than I imagined – after all, I walk past the cars at college every day!'

'I loved that you could choose different sized cars for different trips. It **(5)** *wasn't as good as* owning your own car, it was better!'

'I felt **(6)** *less stressed* knowing I didn't have to pay for expensive repairs.'

Don't delay! Contact us today on register@valleycars.com or visit our website at www.valleycars.com

Comparatives and superlatives

▶ **GRAMMAR** REFERENCE p.127

2 **Match the italic words in Activity 1 with the rules for comparatives and superlatives A–E.**

A Add -*er* and -*est* with short adjectives and adverbs.

B Use *more* and *most* with two-syllable adjectives and adverbs.

C With two-syllable adjectives ending in -*y*, replace the -*y* with -*ier* and -*iest*.

D Add *less* (+ *than*) to mean *a smaller amount*.

E Use *as … as* to mean *to the same degree*.

F Use *not as … as* to mean *a smaller amount*.

LANGUAGE TIP

The comparative and superlative of some adjectives and adverbs are irregular, e.g. *good → better → best*, *bad → worse → worst*, *far → further → furthest*.

3 **Complete the second sentence so that it means the same as the first. Use no more than three words.**

1 It was less stressful than I thought it would be.
It wasn't as stressful as I thought it would be.

2 I don't feel as unfit as I did before.
I feel less unfit than I did before.

3 Living without a car has become much easier.
Living without a car isn't as hard as it was before.

4 I don't spend as much money as before.
I spend less than before.

5 I am more efficient because I can study on the train.
I was less efficient than before I started studying on the train.

6 I thought the system would work better.
The system didn't work as well as I thought it would.

4 **Complete the sentences with a comparative or superlative adjective.**

1 Which do you think is better (*good*): travelling by car or bus?

2 How could travelling around your home town be easier (*easy*)?

3 What's the most (*expensive*) way to travel across your country?

4 What's the most (*unusual*) form of transport you've ever used?

5 Do you think cycling is healthier (*healthy*) than other forms of transport? Why/Why not?

6 What's the furthest (*far*) you've ever travelled?

7 What's the most (*popular*) activity people do to pass time on public transport?

8 Are people in your country more (*careful*) about the environment when they travel these days?

5 **Work in pairs and discuss the questions in Activity 4.**

Speaking

1 Work in pairs. Look at the photos of homes in the two texts and answer the questions.

1 How are the homes different/similar to each other?

2 How similar or different are they to your home?

Reading

Matching (Part 2)

2 Read the advertisement. What is home exchange? Why do people do it?

A home from home

Do you want to see other parts of the world without breaking the bank? Then home exchange could be for you. You live in someone else's house while they live in yours, from a few days to a few weeks.

It's not just about saving money. It gives you a chance to see places that aren't on the tourist map and meet local people.

Visit our home exchange website at www.home-swapit.com. Just add a description of your home, explain where you'd like to stay and find your perfect match.

3 Find expressions in the advert in Activity 2 that mean the same as expressions 1–6.

1 Financial advantages aren't the only reason to do it.

2 Go to our homepage about exchanging homes.

3 Include details about what your home is like.

4 Between a long weekend and a month or so.

5 You have the opportunity to visit locations that holidaymakers don't go to.

6 Say what places you want to go to.

EXAM TIP

Don't match a person with a description because one or two words are repeated. Look for synonyms or expressions which mean the same thing.

4 The people below all want to exchange their homes for one in London for a month. On the opposite page are advertisements for eight homes in London. Decide which home would be the most suitable for the following people.

1 Fernando and Manuela would like to be in a central location where they can enjoy views of the city centre. They are hoping to see several musicals. Manuela doesn't like cats. ▷

2 Ben and Lynne want a house where they can drive to places outside London and learn about how people used to live. Their two sons want to be able to play tennis and go swimming. They don't mind pets.

3 Claire and Tom have two young children. They are an active family who want to see both the countryside and central London. They don't have a car so will need to use other transport. E

4 Anne wants to learn about the history of art and watch plays. She'd like a safe and peaceful home close to the centre. She has pets at home. ◯

5 Andre and Lionel are flatmates. They want to go out dancing and try food from different countries. Exercising regularly is important to them. F

Holiday home eXchange

Enjoy a fantastic city holiday by exchanging your home with one of these fantastic homes in London.

A *Four-bedroom house*
We have a lovely four-bedroom house away from the city centre. There's a **garage**, a **garden** and **antique furniture**. The location offers easy access to several beautiful historical houses by road with a leisure centre and pool just ten minutes away on foot. We have a dog that needs looking after.

B *Modern flat*
I live on the top floor of an old **town house** in a busy street in central London. It's a small but very modern flat with **blinds** and **wooden floors**. There are lots of small art galleries nearby and a bus to Camden market. Just around the corner is a gym.

C *One-bedroom apartment*
I have a quiet one-bedroom flat in the **basement** of a house in central London with good security. It's just two kilometres from the central cultural sites of London, including many theatres and galleries. There's a bus stop just down the road. I have a small black cat to feed.

D *Two-bedroom flat*
We live in a large two-bedroom flat on the third floor of a block in the centre. There's a **balcony**, from which you can see many famous buildings, and luxury **curtains** and **carpets** in all rooms. Several popular London theatres are just a short walk away. We'd rather not have visitors with pets.

E *Large house*
We have a big village house to offer just outside London. It's close to a large train station and Windsor Castle. We have a very large garden for you to relax in during the summer and an open fire and **chimney** for a comfortable winter.

F *Two-bedroom flat*
We live in a secure two-bedroom flat on the twelfth floor with **air conditioning**. Our central, luxury block of flats has a gym and pool. Walk around the corner to find local nightclubs and restaurants serving meals from around the world.

G *Cottage*
We live in a **cottage** opposite a large forest with a beautiful lake where you can try different water sports. You can borrow our bikes to get around the area or take one of the regular trains to the city centre. There are two first floor bedrooms and an **attic** which can be used as a small bedroom.

H *One-bedroom flat*
I have a one-bedroom flat with **central heating** and great views of south London in a quiet, safe street. You can try the European restaurants nearby or take a train to central London. It's close to Wimbledon tennis club and an hour from the coast. A spare **duvet**, **blanket** and a **fan** are available.

Speaking

5 **Work in pairs and answer the questions.**

1 Which house from the website would you like to live in for a month? Why?

2 What's your perfect holiday home like? Describe it.

Vocabulary

House and home

6 **Put the bold words in the advertisement under the correct heading:** *types of houses, parts of a house,* **or** *things you find in a house.*

7 **Complete the sentences with a word/phrase from Activity 6.**

1 I'd prefer to exchange my home for a .... in the city than a .... in the country.

2 I like modern sofas and chairs, not ....

3 I'd rather sleep in the .... at the top of the house than the .... under the house.

4 I like wooden floors more than .... on the floor.

5 I prefer to sleep under a wool .... than a .... with feathers in it.

6 I'd rather have .... to keep cool in summer than .... to keep warm in winter.

8 **Work in pairs. Are the sentences in Activity 7 true for you? Why/Why not?**

Listening

1 **Work in pairs and discuss the questions.**

1 Which English-speaking countries have you visited? Which would you like to visit? Why?

2 Have you ever been on a school exchange programme? What are the advantages and problems with an exchange programme?

2 **Read what three students said about their exchange programme. Decide if each speaker was happy or unhappy.**

A 'I met such interesting people there, even though the town was really small!'

B 'It wasn't warm enough for me. I thought I was going to freeze!'

C 'It was just too wet to do anything. When it rained, everything stopped!'

D 'It was such a big city that there were lots of things to do.'

E 'There were too many tourists passing through.'

F 'I got so good at skiing! I was going down the fast slopes by the end.'

3 ▶ **26 Listen to three people describing their experiences. Which Speaker (1–3) might have said statements A–F in Activity 2?**

too and enough, so and such

▶ **GRAMMAR** REFERENCE p.127

4 **Underline the examples of *too* and *enough* in the sentences in Activity 2 and then complete the rules.**

1 Use ...... before the adjective.

2 Use ...... after the adjective.

5 **Underline the examples of *so*, *such* and *such a* in the sentences in Activity 2, and complete the grammar rules.**

1 Use ...... before an adjective.

2 Use ...... before an adjective + singular noun.

3 Use ...... before an adjective + plural noun or uncountable noun.

LANGUAGE TIP

We use *not enough* and *too* to say that we're unhappy about a situation. *There is **not enough** time to finish the game. I'm **too** tired to go out.*

6 **Choose the correct words to complete the sentences.**

1 There were *enough / too many* students at the college and I didn't enjoy it.

2 My English was *good enough / too good* to be able to communicate.

3 It was hot! I was never *cool enough / too cool* at night!

4 It was *far enough / too far* for me to go.

5 I *didn't have enough / had too much* time to myself.

6 The whole trip was just *short enough / too short*!

7 **Look at Activity 2 and answer the questions.**

1 Which sentences express emphasis?

2 Which sentences express cause and effect?

8 **Complete the second sentence so that it means the same as the first. Use no more than three words.**

1 It'd be such an easy way to learn English.
It'd be .... easy to learn English.

2 I'd be too nervous to sit still on the plane.
I'd be .... that I wouldn't sit still on the plane.

3 My English isn't strong enough to work abroad.
My English is too .... to work abroad.

4 I was so late that I missed applying this year.
I was too late .... this year.

5 I'd miss my friends and family too much to go abroad.
I'd miss my friends .... that I couldn't go abroad.

9 **Imagine an exchange student wants to come to your home town. How would you describe it? Write your own ideas then tell a partner.**

1 My home town is such a…

2 It doesn't really have enough…

3 The weather is so…

4 There are too many/is too much…

Reading

 1 You receive this email from your future exchange partner in the United States. Read it and answer the questions.

1 Where do you think Beth lives?

2 What does she want you to bring? Why?

3 What activity is she suggesting?

> ▶ Search
>
> Hi Javier
>
> Just a quick reminder – don't forget to bring a torch with you next month. In January, the sun won't rise until the 23rd of the month, so it'll be dark while you're here. I was thinking about things we could do together. My dad goes out on 'polar bear watch' every night, to make sure they don't come into town. One ate a plateful of reindeer burgers from a barbecue last month. Why don't we join him one night? It'll be fun!
>
> Lots of love
> Beth

2 Work in pairs and discuss the questions.

1 Do you think it would be interesting to do an exchange with Beth? Why/Why not?

2 Would you want to do the activity she's suggesting?

Writing

Message (Part 2)

▶ **WRITING** REFERENCE p.139

3 Look at the task and answer the questions.

1 What three things do you need to do?

2 How many words do you need to write?

> Your exchange partner has arranged an activity to do together but you don't want to do it.
> Write an email to your exchange partner. In your email you should
> • explain why you don't want to do the activity.
> • apologise for not accepting the offer.
> • suggest a different activity.
> Write **35–45 words**.

EXAM TIP

It is important that you do all three things in the instructions. If you forget one of the content points, you will get a lower mark.

4 Look at the sample answer below and answer the questions. Then correct Javier's email.

1 Has Javier done all three things in the instructions?

2 What does Javier need to add to improve the email?

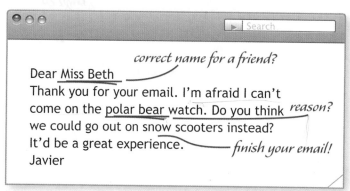

> ▶ Search
>
> *correct name for a friend?*
> Dear Miss Beth
> Thank you for your email. I'm afraid I can't come on the polar bear watch. Do you think *reason?* we could go out on snow scooters instead? It'd be a great experience. *finish your email!*
> Javier

5 Look at the task below and follow steps 1–4.

1 Think of some ideas.

2 Make notes.

3 Write your email.

4 Check you have covered all the points.

> You visited your exchange partner's family last month, and now your partner is coming to stay with you.
> Write an email to your exchange partner. In your email you should
> • tell your partner about the meeting arrangements.
> • ask him or her about any food that they don't like.
> • suggest an activity you can do together.
> Write **35–45 words**.

You live and learn

Speaking

1 Work in pairs. How has the way you learn changed since you were a child? What effects have changes in technology had on this?

Reading
Multiple choice (Part 4)

2 Read the questions and 'skim' the blog. What's it about?

Learning English

The News

Blog feed All feeds

HOME NEWS WORLD SPORT FINANCE **COMMENT** BLOGS CULTURE TRAVEL LIFE FASHION   Dating Offers Jobs

English dot com

Adapted from an article by Tomasz P. Szynalski

When you hear how I learned a foreign language, you have to remember a few things. In 1993, when I was starting to learn English, no one had heard of the internet. I wasn't able to read websites on topics that I found interesting or follow blogs. And I have no idea how I decided which movies to see without my favourite movie review website.

My reading practice was limited to literature. All I had were the few books **on sale** locally, plus whatever I could get from my cousin in America. For listening practice, I only had the news and cartoons on cable TV. DVDs didn't exist **at all**. People bought and rented VHS videos but in Poland there was no spoken English on them. The only way to hear that was to visit the movies.

My dictionaries were all in book form until I received my first PC dictionary. It came on **at least** six disks and had unhelpful explanations and few example sentences. It doesn't sound very useful but **in fact** I loved it, **because of** its ability to work with other programs and find English words more quickly. Today, computerised dictionaries have simple explanations and lots of examples.

If I were a complete beginner learning English today, I'd spend hours on the web, reading about my favourite topics, downloading **up to date** movies, emailing English-speaking friends and posting comments on forums. Yes, I admit, **at first** it would probably be hard to understand real-life English, but I'd spend time looking things up and **in the end** I'm sure I'd pick up the language much faster than I did back in 1993.

---

3 Read the text again and answer the questions below. For each question choose the correct answer A–D.

1 What is Tomasz trying to do in the text?

A Encourage people to start learning a foreign language.

B Complain about the use of technology in language learning.

C Explain how language learning materials have changed.

D Compare two different ways of teaching a language.

2 Tomasz says he doesn't know

A how he used to choose films to watch.

B when he first heard about the internet.

C where he bought English books online from.

D which topics he found interesting.

3 To watch films in English, Polish people in the 1990s had to

A rent films on videotape.

B watch TV for children.

C have cable television.

D go to the cinema.

4 Tomasz liked his first computer dictionary because it

A found information at a faster speed.

B gave you useful example sentences.

C was better than today's dictionaries.

D came with other computer programs.

5 Which of these might Tomasz say about learning English through the internet?

A It was more interesting to learn a language when you had to work hard to find materials to study with.

B You'll need someone to help you to begin with but eventually you'll learn English more quickly.

C It's a great way to improve your English because you can find things online that interest you.

D If you study English through books, you learn more useful vocabulary than when you study online.

Speaking

4 Work in pairs. How can the internet help you improve the areas in the box? Which of the activities do you do?

| listening | vocabulary | reading |
| grammar | speaking | writing |

Vocabulary

Prepositional phrases

5 Match the phrases in bold from the blog with the definitions 1–8.

1 .... means *not less than*.

2 .... introduces surprising but true information.

3 .... means *modern* or *recent*.

4 .... is used to give a reason for something.

5 .... means *available to buy*.

6 .... means *at the beginning*.

7 .... means *not even slightly*.

8 .... means *finally*.

6 Complete the sentences with a prepositional phrase from Activity 5.

1 I wasn't keen on learning English .... but now I love it.

2 I used to think blogging was boring. .... it's a lot of fun.

3 When I buy books online, I have to pay .... £5 for postage.

4 I love watching comedies in English but I don't like documentaries ....

5 There's one website I always go to for .... news.

6 I thought about moving abroad to learn English. .... I decided not to.

7 There are some English magazines .... at my local supermarket.

8 I really enjoy going on internet forums .... the humour.

7 Work in pairs. Are the sentences in Activity 6 true for you? Why/Why not? Can you change the untrue sentences so they are true for you?

Listening

1 **Work in pairs and answer the questions.**

1 Is it important to learn new things throughout your life? Why/Why not?

2 What new skill would you like to learn? Why?

2 ▶ 27 **Listen to a telephone conversation between two friends, George and Jo. Why is George calling?**

3 **Listen again. Decide if each sentence is correct or incorrect.**

1 Jo said she wanted to take an evening course.

2 It was free for the audience to watch the end-of-course performance.

3 George saw a friend perform well.

4 Course lessons are once a week for four weeks.

5 George believes that difficult things are more rewarding.

6 Jo agrees to do the course with George.

Speaking

4 **Work in pairs and answer the questions.**

1 Would you like to attend this course? Why/Why not?

2 What skills do you need to tell a joke well?

3 Do you think that people from other countries understand jokes from your country? Why/Why not?

Past simple and past continuous

▶ **GRAMMAR** REFERENCE p.128

5 **Look at sentences A–C from the conversation and answer the questions.**

A As I was looking for the football results, I saw an ad for a comedy course.

B A friend of mine took a similar course a couple of years ago.

C While he was telling his jokes, the audience were talking!

1 Which sentence describes one completed past action? B

2 Which sentence describes a past action in progress when another action happened? A

3 Which sentence describes two past actions in progress at the same time? C

LANGUAGE TIP

We can use *while*, *as* or *when* to show that two past actions happened at the same time. The *while*, *as* or *when* clause can come at the beginning or end of the sentence.

6 ▶ 28 **Listen to sentence C from Activity 5. How are *was* and *were* pronounced?**

7 **Work in pairs. Student A, turn to page 120. Student B, put the verbs in brackets into the correct past simple or past continuous form. Check your answers with another Student B.**

Driving Penguins

A man **(1)** .... (*drive*) some penguins to a zoo when his lorry **(2)** .... (*break*) down. While he **(3)** .... (*examine*) the engine, another lorry driver **(4)** .... (*stop*) to help. The first driver explained he **(5)** .... (*take*) the penguins to the zoo and his boss would be angry if he didn't do it. He **(6)** .... (*offer*) the other driver £100 to take them instead. The second driver **(7)** .... (*agree*) and **(8)** .... (*take*) the money.

Three hours later, the first lorry driver **(9)** .... (*still/sit*) at the side of the road when the second lorry driver **(10)** .... (*drive*) past with a penguin in the front seat. The first driver shouted at him to stop, so he did. 'I **(11)** .... (*ask*) you to take the penguins to the zoo for me,' the first driver said. 'I did,' said the second driver, 'but I **(12)** .... (*have*) some money left over, so now I'm taking them to the cinema.'

8 **Student A and Student B work together. Tell each other your jokes. Which is the funniest?**

Speaking

1 **Work in pairs and discuss the questions.**

1 What kind of school student were you?

2 What did your teachers say about you in your school reports?

Education

2 **Quickly read the extracts from George's school reports. Which stage of education is each report for?**

A Basically, George is keen on building things. He takes great pleasure in creating bridges and knocking them down. He can use a pen well, and is very good at drawing simple pictures, although he finds it hard to concentrate on reading. (aged 5)

B Broadly speaking, George needs to pay more attention in class. He's continually talking with other students and puts considerably more effort into playing around than revising for exams. I suggest he register for extra classes. However, he worked hard on his model pyramid for the Egyptian project, and has made good progress in maths. (aged 15)

C George hasn't been able to attend every class, which is a pity. However, he clearly has a good understanding of the technical side of his subject and has achieved good grades when his teachers set homework. His final project, a design for a new library, was originally based on his drawings from childhood. It was easily among the best projects we received. (aged 21)

3 **Read questions 1–6. Underline the italic phrases in George's school reports. Then try to guess what the phrases mean.**

1 Which subjects did you *find it hard to concentrate* on?

2 When *teachers set homework*, do you always do it? Why/Why not?

3 Do you *attend every class*? Why/Why not?

4 Do you think you've *made good progress in* your English? Why/Why not?

5 Would you like to *register for* evening classes? Why/Why not? Which one?

6 Do you find *revising for exams* or tests difficult?

4 **Work in pairs and discuss the questions in Activity 3.**

Adverbs

5 **Underline the adverbs in the texts in Activity 2. Then complete sentences 1–8 with an adverb with a similar meaning to the phrase in brackets.**

1 I couldn't really concentrate because he was .... asking questions. (*all the time*)

2 This classroom was .... used as an office. (*in the beginning*)

3 I tried really .... to pass the test. (*with a lot of effort*)

4 .... my sister refused to come on the course. (*to give a simple explanation*)

5 We did our projects on .... similar topics. (*in a general way*)

6 My partner looked confused and .... didn't understand. (*without any doubt*)

7 He never does any work, but he .... gets the highest grades. (*without difficulty*)

8 I had .... more free time after I finished my course. (*enough to be important*)

LANGUAGE TIP

George works hard means George works a lot. *George hardly works* means he works very little.

Speaking

6 **Work in pairs and discuss the questions.**

1 What job do you think George does now? Why?

2 Do you think school reports are a good prediction of how well children will do in future? Why/Why not?

7 **Work in pairs. Student A, look at the report on page 121. Student B, look at the report on page 122. Follow the instructions.**

Speaking

1 **Work in pairs and discuss the questions.**

1 Why do people go to school?

2 What kind of things did you learn at primary school? What did you enjoy most at primary school?

3 What things did you enjoy the most/least about secondary school?

2 **Work in pairs. How can people learn these skills?**

1 successful communication

2 being good with money

3 good dress sense

4 living healthily

5 decision-making

6 time management

Listening

True/False (Part 4)

EXAM TIP

Listen for words and phrases with a similar meaning to those used in the question.

3 **You will hear a woman called Suzie and a man called Gus talking about the things they learnt during their twenties. Before you listen, read sentences 1–6 and underline the key words. Think of other ways to say the key words.**

		A	B
1	At first Gus was worried about finishing university.	☐	☐
2	Suzie's friends changed careers several times in their twenties.	☐	☐
3	Suzie regrets her decision to work as a waitress.	☐	☐
4	Gus found it difficult to make changes to his lifestyle after university.	☐	☐
5	They agree that it can be helpful to compare yourself to others.	☐	☐
6	In his twenties, Gus expected problems to disappear quickly.	☐	☐

4 ▶ **29 Listen to the recording. Decide if each sentence is correct or incorrect. If it is correct, put a tick (✓) in the box under A for YES. If it is not correct, put a tick (✓) in the box under B for NO.**

Speaking

5 **Work in pairs and discuss the questions.**

1 Do you think many people in their twenties feel the same way as Gus and Suzie? Why/Why not?

2 What do you think are the good and bad things about being in your early teens, late teens, twenties and older?

3 What do you think is the best age to be? Why?

Speaking

1 **Look at the advert. Work in pairs and discuss the questions.**

1 Would you like to work with young people?

2 What do you think you could teach well?

3 What kind of values or qualities do teachers often want to pass on to young people?

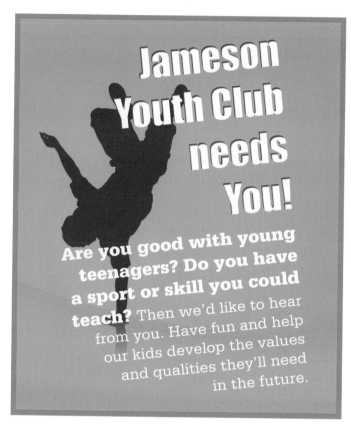

Jameson Youth Club needs You!

Are you good with young teenagers? Do you have a sport or skill you could teach? Then we'd like to hear from you. Have fun and help our kids develop the values and qualities they'll need in the future.

Personal questions (Part 1)

2 ▶ 30 **Listen to the manager of the youth club talking to two people who are interested in working there. Which speaker would you choose to work at the centre? Why?**

3 ▶ 31 **Listen to Speaker 2 again and complete the conversation.**

1 .... I guess working with kids is going to be a challenge, but it'll be a great experience and, ... , I'm good with kids.

2 I think a lot of kids are interested in street dance and, ... , it's a good way to get them fit and keep them busy in the evenings.

3 That's why I think street dance is so good. .... , they have to learn to be responsible and work hard, even in their free time.

4 **Write the words or phrases from Activity 2 in the best place in the table below.**

pausing	like, ... , ...
changing topic	mind you, ...
giving an honest answer	as a matter of fact, ...

EXAM TIP

You will sound more natural and fluent if you use discourse markers (words that tell the listener how you feel or where the conversation is going) in your speech.

5 **Work in groups of three. Student A turn to page 120, Student B turn to page 121, and Student C turn to page 122. Follow the instructions.**

Speaking

1 Work in pairs. Do you think there are different types of intelligence? Why/Why not?

Reading

2 Read the article about Kim Ung-Yong and answer the questions.

1 What did Kim learn before he was two?
2 What did Kim finish before he was 16?
3 How long did he spend at NASA before he left the USA?
4 What did Kim do before he started his planning job?

6:23   @ 67% 🔋

Issues   **Sections**   Settings

Kim Ung-Yong: a failed genius?

One of the most intelligent people in the world is Korean engineer Kim Ung-Yong, who has an IQ of 210. **(1)** By the time Kim <u>was</u> two he'd <u>learnt</u> to read four languages. He could solve complex maths problems aged four and **(2)** <u>had already attended</u> university classes for three years when he <u>turned</u> seven.

(3) By the time he <u>celebrated</u> his 16th birthday, he'd spent four years working for NASA in the USA, and <u>had completed</u> a physics PhD. However, he missed his family, so soon returned home. He decided to change direction and study engineering. Although he was offered a place at a top university, he chose to attend his local university instead.

(4) After he'<u>d graduated</u> with his second PhD, he <u>started</u> work at the planning department of a medium-sized development company, where he still works today. Kim believes his life to be successful, but the Korean media has criticised his career choices, calling him a 'failed genius'.

3 Work in pairs and discuss the questions.

1 Are you surprised by Kim's choices? Why/Why not?
2 Were the Korean media right to criticise his choices? Why/Why not?

Past perfect simple

▶ **GRAMMAR** REFERENCE p.128

4 Look at the two underlined verb forms in each sentence 1–4 in the article and answer the questions.

1 Which action happened first in each sentence?
2 What verb form is used to describe the action that happened first?

LANGUAGE TIP

We use the past perfect to talk about a past action which happened before another past action.

5 Complete the sentences by putting the verbs in brackets into the correct past simple or past perfect form.

1 By the time Christopher Langan .... (*be*) three years old, he .... (*teach*) himself to read.
2 By the time chess player Judit Polgár .... (*be*) 16, she .... (*become*) an International Grandmaster, the highest position in the game.
3 Alia Sabur .... (*already/become*) the world's youngest university professor when she .... (*turn*) 19.
4 Andrew Wiles .... (*already/solve*) one of the most difficult maths problems in the world by the time he .... (*start*) secondary school.
5 When Christopher Hirata .... (*celebrate*) his 16th birthday, he .... (*already/start*) working for NASA.
6 Akrit Jaswal .... (*manage*) to perform his first operation aged seven because he .... (*read*) lots of books about it.

Speaking

6 You are going to talk about someone you consider to be a successful person. Make notes about

1 the name of the person and the person's background.
2 what the person had achieved by the time he/she finished school and was in his/her twenties/thirties/forties, etc.
3 why you think the person was successful.
4 why you admire the person.

7 Work in pairs. Take turns to tell each other about the person in Activity 6. Who do you think is the most successful person?

Writing
Story (Part 3)
▶ **WRITING** REFERENCE p.141

1 **Read this exam task. Have you ever had a lucky escape? What happened?**

Your English teacher has asked you to write a story. Your story must begin with this sentence:
It was such a lucky escape!
Write your **story** in about **100 words**.

2 **Work with a partner. What could be your escape from each of these situations?**

1 bad weather
2 being told off
3 certain death

3 **Read one student's lucky escape story and answer the questions.**

1 Why was the boy going to fail the test?
2 Why do you think the boy put his exam paper in the middle, and ran at the end?

THE GREAT EXAM ESCAPE
It was such a lucky escape! Before the exam had started, the strict chemistry professor had warned the students, 'If you continue to write after the bell, you'll score zero.'
   The hour finished, but one boy carried on writing. 'You've failed!' the professor said, but the boy was surprisingly calm. 'Do you know who I am?' he asked.
   The professor explained very slowly, 'It doesn't matter if you're the President's son, you've still failed.'
   'But you don't know?' the boy continued. By this time the professor was getting annoyed. 'I don't know and I don't care!'
   The boy smiled hid his paper in the middle of the pile of exams and ran out of the room.

4 **Work in pairs and answer the questions about the student answer.**

1 What's the purpose of each paragraph?
2 What verb forms are used to a) set the scene, b) tell the main story and c) end the story?
3 What adverbs and adjectives are used to add interest?

EXAM TIP
Continue a story from a sentence by using the past perfect to set the scene. Then use the past simple and continuous to tell the main story and end the story.

5 **Read another student's answer and put the verbs in brackets into the correct past perfect, continuous or simple form.**

The Trip to the Café
It was such a lucky escape. Two Australian students (1) .... (spend) the morning surfing. They (2) .... (plan) to stay near the beach, but the waves (3) .... (get) bigger. Suddenly, they realised that while they (4) .... (watch) the other surfers, the waves (5) .... (push) them towards the rocks.
   They panicked! The locals (6) .... (warn) them about that area. They (7) .... (try) to swim away when a huge wave (8) .... (pull) them down under the water. When they finally (9) .... (come) back up, they (10) .... (be) inside a cave. Looking around, they (11) .... (notice) that someone (12) .... (build) some steps at the back of the cave.
   They (13) .... (climb) up, and (14) .... (reach) a door. When a woman (15) .... (open) it, they were amazed to find themselves in the tourist café at the top of the cliff.

6 **Now write your answer to the exam task in Activity 1. Think about the things in Activity 4 that you can include to get a higher mark.**

PROGRESS TEST 3

1 Put the adjectives in brackets in the correct order.

1 I want to buy that .... coat. *(black, leather, long)*

2 Have you seen my .... bag? *(green, plastic, big)*

3 That's a .... watch. *(gold, lovely, thin)*

4 I can't find my .... tie anywhere. *(expensive, silk, blue)*

5 Elena's just bought a .... jumper. *(woollen, white, beautiful)*

6 Greg's wearing his .... shirt. *(cotton, horrible, orange)*

2 Decide if these sentences are grammatically correct or incorrect. Correct the ones that are incorrect.

1 My brother lives in the biggest house in the street.

2 This hotel isn't expensive as that one.

3 It's sunnier than it was this morning.

4 If you walk more fast, we'll get there more soon.

5 I want to swap my car for one that's less noisier.

6 I don't feel as ill as I did last night.

7 That jacket is the horriblest thing I've ever seen!

8 Your driving is worser than it used to be!

9 This shirt is a brighter colour that one.

10 It's more convenient for us to get the bus into town.

3 Write the nouns that are being described.

1 A room in a house below ground level. b........................

2 A room at the very top of a house. a........................

3 Material on the floor of a house that goes from wall to wall. c........................

4 A pipe which takes fire smoke out of a house, through the roof. c........................

5 A system which makes heat in one place and sends it around a building. c........................ h........................

6 A traditional country house. c........................

7 Old, valuable tables and chairs. a........................ f........................

8 Pieces of material you pull across to cover a window. c........................

9 A system that makes the air in a room or building stay cool. a........................ c........................

10 A thick warm bed cover. d........................

4 Read Ana's opinions about shopping and choose the correct words.

'I can't stand going clothes shopping at the weekend. It takes (1) *so / such* a long time to find what you want because the shops are (2) *so / such* crowded. The changing rooms aren't big (3) *enough / too* for everyone so you have to wait ages and the sales people are (4) *so / too* busy to help you. Then there are (5) *so / such* long queues at the checkout that it takes 15 minutes just to pay. I'm (6) *enough / too* impatient and usually just give up and leave without buying anything.'

5 Complete the sentences with an appropriate preposition.

1 There aren't any blankets .... sale at the department store.

2 I really don't like this coffee .... all.

3 There are .... least five people waiting for the train, maybe more.

4 There's hardly any traffic on the roads because .... the snow.

5 Have you got an .... to date bus timetable?

6 .... first I didn't like Jimmy, but now I think he's great!

6 Match the first half of the sentences about Sami's experience at a language school in the USA with the second half.

1 Josie chose to register

2 She attended

3 However, she often found it

4 Her teacher set the class

5 She revised

6 She easily

7 Her teacher told her she had made good

8 When she left the USA, she was considerably

A got a high grade.

B difficult to concentrate after lunch.

C more confident than when she had arrived.

D homework every day.

E every one of her lessons.

F for both morning and afternoon classes.

G hard for the end of course exam.

H progress in her English.

7 Read about Antony's travel experience. Put the verb in brackets in the past simple, past continuous or past perfect simple tense.

When I was in my late teens my friend and I **(1)** ...decided... (decide) to go backpacking across Europe. With the railcards that we **(2)** ...had bought... (buy) a month earlier in our bags, we **(3)** ...said... (say) goodbye to our parents and **(4)** ...went... (go) to the train station. Then, while we **(5)** ...were waiting... (wait) for the Paris train to arrive, I **(6)** ...looked... (look) in my backpack to make sure that I **(7)** ...had packed... (pack) my passport. Unfortunately the bag **(8)** ...fell... (fall) from my hands onto the train tracks. That wasn't the worst thing, though, because my clothes **(9)** ...fell out... (fall out) of my bag and **(10)** ...were lying... (lie) on the tracks for everyone to see. That included my underwear!

8 Look at the pairs of sentences about unusual schools. Complete the second sentence so it means the same as the first. Use no more than three words.

1 Students at mountain schools spend more time skiing than studying traditional subjects.

At mountain schools, students don't spend ...as much time... studying traditional subjects as they do skiing.

2 In forest schools, the children have such a lot of fun learning outside.

In forest schools, the children have so ...much... chance learning outside.

3 Last year, students studied at 'space camp' summer school and created a robot.

While students ...were studying... at 'space camp' summer school, they created a robot.

4 It is obvious that people go to spy school to learn to be spies.

People ...obviously... go to spy school to learn to be spies.

5 Because London's very historical, it's a good place to learn to be a ghost hunter.

London is a good place to learn to be a ghost hunter ...because... its history.

6 The students studied at circus school for a year before they got a job at a circus.

By the time the students got a job at a circus, they ...have been... at circus school for a year.

9 Read the text below and choose the correct word for each space. Choose the correct answer A–D.

Learning Zone • ISSUE 18

Memory and learning

Think about the last English lesson you had. While you **(1)** .... studying, did you feel hungry or thirsty? Were you **(2)** .... warm? Was the sun in your eyes? If so, then you probably found it harder to concentrate than normal and the learning was possibly **(3)** .... effective. It's great to **(4)** .... every class but if you don't pay attention while you're there, then you won't learn. Eat and drink before class and carry an extra jumper to **(5)** .... if it's cold so you can focus. Pull the **(6)** .... down on the windows so it's not too bright.

It's a sad fact that we remember little information we hear. In **(7)** .... , we forget around 80 percent of the information we learn so we have to work **(8)** .... to remember it. Revising information is **(9)** .... an important activity for a language learner because a memory only becomes strong with practice. Using the language as much as possible will help you make good **(10)** ....

1	**A** were	**B** had	**C** are	**D** have
2	**A** so	**B** enough	**C** such	**D** too
3	**A** as	**B** least	**C** much	**D** less
4	**A** register	**B** attend	**C** go	**D** stay
5	**A** put on	**B** hang up	**C** try on	**D** wear out
6	**A** duvet	**B** blankets	**C** curtains	**D** blinds
7	**A** half	**B** order	**C** front	**D** fact
8	**A** hardly	**B** hard	**C** basic	**D** basically
9	**A** so	**B** such	**C** too	**D** enough
10	**A** progress	**B** development	**C** direction	**D** work

Water

7

Speaking

1 Work in pairs and discuss. How do you use water every day? How much do you think you use?

2 Look at the box. How much water do you think each activity needs?

a bath   a ten-minute shower   drinking water for one day
cooking a meal   washing towels

3 ▶ 32 Listen and check your answers to Activity 2.

Listening
Multiple choice (Part 2)

EXAM TIP

If there's a word that you don't understand in the questions, circle it and carry on. Then once you have read all the questions, try and guess the meaning.

4 ▶ 33 Listen to a student called Jessica talking about how a cruise ship uses water. For each question, choose the correct answer A–C.

1 Jessica chose to talk about the Ocean Star because it
   A   has so many people on board.
   B   is very responsible environmentally.
   C   uses so little water every day.

2 What does Jessica say uses the most water on cruise ships?
   A   baths and showers   B   drinks   C   cooling food

3 The showers worked efficiently because
   A   the shower heads had more holes.
   B   the water came out so fast.
   C   there was a time limit on them.

4 The best thing about the swimming pool water was
   A   that it was easy to keep clean.
   B   that it was mostly sea water.
   C   that it didn't need dangerous products.

5 The water from the air conditioning was used for

   A watering plants.   **B** washing towels.

   C cleaning the rooms.

6 Data collected by Ocean Star is sent to

   A universities.   **B** environmental groups.

   C local governments.

Countable and uncountable nouns

▶ **GRAMMAR** REFERENCE p.128

5 Work in pairs. Look at the advert for a cruise and answer the questions.

1 Would you go on this kind of cruise? Why/Why not?

2 Where in the world would you like to sail?

Top Cruises with

Ocean Star

Wake up to the luxury of an Ocean Star experience in one of our many five-star, ocean-view bedrooms.

Start your day with a little caviar on toast and end it with our midnight chocolate buffet. In between, order food from our amazing restaurant at any time of the day. There isn't much chance you'll go hungry on our **ship**.

We also have waiter service by the pool – enjoy relaxing with some **fruit juice** and a few olives – we have six pools to choose from!

Our main **pool** is over 150 **metres** long, and has over 2 million **litres** of crystal clear **water**, and we offer classes in **surfing**, aqua aerobics and **scuba diving**.

In the evenings, you'll love our concert hall, which can hold 2,000 people. Choose from concerts by top **rock artists**, or come and listen to your favourite television **chefs** sharing their expert **advice**. Our crew speak several languages including **English**, **Spanish** and Chinese and will be happy to help. Your **comfort** is our business. So what are you waiting for?

www.oceanstargalaxy.com

6 Look at the table. Add the words in bold from Activity 5 to the chart, then add one more to each list.

normally countable nouns	
1 people, animals and plants	a teacher, a dog, a rose, ... , ...
2 objects	a bottle, a desk, ... , ...
3 units of measurement	a kilometre, a kilogramme, ... , ...

normally uncountable nouns	
4 materials, liquids or gases	smoke, steam, ... , ...
5 activities	camping, eating, ... , ...
6 languages	English, ... , ...
7 abstract nouns	beauty, love, ... , ...

7 Complete the rules with the words in the box. Use the examples of *a few, a little, many* and *much* in the text to help you.

Use .... and .... with countable nouns.

Use .... and .... with uncountable nouns.

We can use *a lot of* or *lots of* with either countable or uncountable nouns.

LANGUAGE TIP

Use *a lot of* in positive sentences, and *much* and *many* in negative sentences, or in a positive sentence after the word *so*.

8 Turn to page 114 for more practice with *a few, a little, many* and *much*.

9 Some words can be both countable and uncountable. Choose the correct words to complete the sentences.

1 **A** The engines didn't make *a noise/noise*!

   B *A noise/Noise* is the last thing you want on holiday.

2 **A** *A painting/Painting* was a relaxing way to spend the afternoon.

   B I bought *a painting/painting* when we stopped on shore.

3 **A** I didn't have a *time/time* to sleep much.

   B It was a *time/time* I'll never forget.

4 **A** I started every morning with *a glass/glass* of fresh orange juice.

   B *A glass/Glass* lets you see more of the amazing views.

10 Work in pairs. Turn to page 123 and follow the instructions.

Weather

1 Work in pairs and complete the quiz with words from the list.

driest	highest	ice	lightning
lowest	snowfall	sunniest	
sunshine	wettest	windiest	

Weathering the storm

How well do you know your weather?
Complete these weather facts and find out!

1 A village in India is the .... place in the world.
2 Antofagasta in Chile is the .... place.
3 Libya had the .... ever recorded temperature.
4 Antarctica had the .... ever recorded temperature.
5 Commonwealth Bay in Antarctica is the .... place.
6 The South Pole has the least ....
7 The place with the most .... is a village in central Africa.
8 Yuma, Arizona, USA is the .... place.
9 Mount Baker in Washington had the heaviest .... in one year.
10 The largest piece of .... fell during a storm in South Dakota, USA.

> Score 8–10: Brilliant! You've taken this quiz by storm.
> 4–7: Not bad but you seem to be in a bit of a fog.
> 1–3: You're obviously feeling under the weather today.
> Read more details in our feature article on page 216.

2 ▶ 34 Listen and check your answers.

3 Why were these numbers mentioned? Listen again and check your answers.

26	300,000	1922	–89.2
182	4,000	30	2010

LANGUAGE TIP

–89.2°C is pronounced *minus eighty-nine point two degrees centigrade*.

4 Complete the weather forecast with the words from the list.

blowing	centigrade	low	cool
dry	fog	frost	gales	mild
showers	sunny	thunderstorms	

There'll be a cold start for those of you in Scotland this morning as you wake up to **(1)** .... on the ground. There'll be **(2)** .... in some areas, making it difficult to see while driving. This will clear by lunchtime but temperatures will stay **(3)** .... at around 3° **(4)** .... In the north of England it'll be cloudy and **(5)** .... for most of the day with some **(6)** .... during the afternoon. Good news for our gardens!

There'll be **(7)** .... temperatures for this time of year in the south of England and Wales, between 10 and 14°C, and it'll be **(8)** .... and **(9)** .... for most of the day. In Northern Ireland there'll be strong **(10)** .... across much of the country, with winds **(11)** .... up to 70mph in some areas. Tomorrow won't be much better, with rain and **(12)** .... expected from the west, so keep your pets inside.

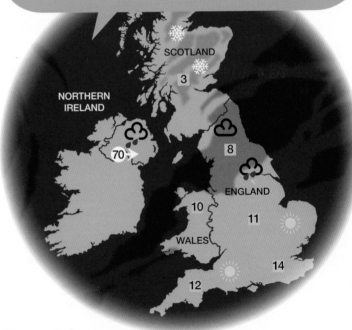

SCOTLAND
3
NORTHERN IRELAND
70
8
ENGLAND
10
11
WALES
14
12

Speaking

5 Work in pairs and discuss the questions.

1 How is the climate different in the regions of your country?
2 How does the climate change in different seasons?
3 Do you think the climate of a country affects people's character or social activities?

Speaking
Simulated situation (Part 2)

1 **Work in pairs. Look at the photos and discuss the questions.**

1 Have you ever entered a race? What happened?
2 Do you think you would be good at these races? Why/ Why not?
3 Do you have unusual races like this in your country?

2 ▶ 35 **Listen to two people discussing what equipment to take for the Maldon Mud Race shown in Picture A. Which three things do they agree are the most important? How does the man encourage the woman to say more?**

drink	jumper	swimming costume
shorts	trainers	trousers	T-shirt

EXAM TIP

It's important that you encourage your partner to talk. If your partner *still* does not say much, your own grade is not affected.

3 **Complete statements 1–4 so they are true for you.**

1 .... is my favourite activity.
2 I prefer to .... on Sunday afternoons.
3 I .... regularly.
4 I do more .... now than I did in the past.

4 **Work in pairs. Take turns to listen to your partner's statements. Then ask follow-up questions with the prompts in the box.**

Why…	Who…	When…	What…
Where…	What other…		

5 **Look at the compound nouns describing objects you might need in the Siberian Ice Marathon, a race through snow-covered Siberia in winter. Match the words to a picture and underline the stress in the words.**

woolly hat	ski gloves	water bottle
energy bars	sunglasses	T-shirt
snow shoes		

6 **Work in pairs.**

You are preparing for the Siberian Ice Marathon. Talk together about the different things you could take with you, and decide which three things would be most important. Use the ideas in Activity 4 to help you.

7 **Work in pairs and discuss the questions.**

1 What's the most difficult physical challenge you've ever experienced?
2 Why do people like difficult challenges?
3 Whose responsibility should it be to rescue people who get in trouble doing dangerous activities in your country?

A

B

Speaking

1 **Work in pairs and discuss the questions.**

1 In what ways can water be good for your health?

2 Have you ever been to a health spa? Would you like to? Why/Why not?

Reading

True/False (Part 3)

2 **You are going to read a brochure. Read sentences 1–10 first. What is the brochure for?**

		A	B
1	Japanese hot water baths are located in cities.	☒	☒
2	People come to the spa for different reasons.	☐	☒
3	The high temperature of the Hydrotherapy Bath can stop you becoming ill.	☑	☒
4	A Hydrotherapy Bath is always made with mineral water.	☐	☑
5	The Floating Pool Experience takes four hours.	☐	☑
6	The only product used in a Sea Salt Bath is sea salt.	☑	☐
7	More than one Cleopatra Bath is necessary to experience good results.	☑	☐
8	Watsu® movements can only be done in water.	☐	☒
9	The spa has facilities for outdoor sports.	☑	☐
10	You have to pay extra for lunch during your stay.	☐	☑

3 **Read the article quickly to see if your prediction was correct.**

4 **Look at sentence 1 in Activity 2. Read the first paragraph of the advertisement. Is the sentence correct or incorrect? What words give you the answer?**

EXAM TIP

Don't worry if you see some words in the text you don't know. Focus on finding the information you need.

5 **Now read the rest of the text to decide if each sentence in Activity 2 is correct or incorrect. If it is correct, mark A. If it is incorrect, mark B.**

Vocabulary

adjectives + prepositions

6 **Complete questions 1–12 with the correct prepositions. The adjectives and prepositions are all in the advertisement.**

How many students in the class...

1 have visited a place which is *famous* .... some kind of water?

2 are *attracted* .... the spa in the advert?

3 feel better .... doing sports?

4 have been to a spa *similar* .... the one in the advert?

5 are *tired* .... feeling stressed?

6 are *ready* .... some relaxation?

7 are *familiar* .... different relaxation techniques?

8 are *amazed* .... the different kinds of facilities at the spa?

9 are *keen* .... having a Cleopatra Bath?

10 are *fond* .... very hot baths?

11 have been *involved* .... water sport activities in the past?

12 are *interested* .... trying Watsu®?

7 **Choose one question from Activity 6. Interview all the students in the class to find out the answer.**

NEW FOREST HEALTH SPA

The use of water to improve our health has been around for centuries. The Romans had their bathhouses. Turkey is famous for its steam baths and in Japan, stressed city workers regularly travel out of town at weekends to relax at the natural hot water baths.

Now you too can enjoy the health benefits of water. Thousands of people from a variety of backgrounds have been attracted to our award-winning spa since it opened in 2002 but they all have one thing in common – they're ready for the relaxation of both body and mind.

Our facilities

One of our most popular facilities is the Hydrotherapy Bath. Similar to a jacuzzi, water shoots out of the bottom and sides of the bath to help you to feel relaxed. As your body temperature increases in the hot water, your blood flows more easily which can prevent you from getting sick. On request, we can fill your bath with mineral water for even greater benefits to your skin.

If you are tired of the noise and activity that fill your daily life, then try our Floating Pool Experience. You lie quietly in a shallow pool of warm salt water in a dark room with nothing but silence around you. Your one hour in this pool will give you the same rest as four hours' sleep.

If you are worried about dry, hard skin then try our Sea Salt Bath. We will cover your body with salt from the Dead Sea and leave you to lie quietly in a steam room for an hour.

Our Cleopatra Bath is the ultimate body luxury. Full of warm horse's milk, the bath leaves your skin feeling like silk. However, three 30-minute sessions are recommended for the full benefits to be felt.

Finally, you cannot leave our spa without trying Watsu®. As you lie in a warm pool, an expert will gently move and stretch your body into different positions that are not possible on land. This experience can make your body stronger and remove stress.

About us

For those of you familiar with the area, you will know that our spa is set in the most beautiful part of the New Forest. We offer five star accommodation and a luxury restaurant. Active guests will be amazed by our indoor swimming pool, gym, grass tennis courts and horse riding facilities. If you are keen on a morning run or fond of cycling, you can use our beautiful gardens or the nearby forest. Everyone is welcome to get involved in our daily exercise classes. Our spa weekend begins each Friday at 2 p.m. with afternoon tea and ends at midday on Sunday. The price is £350 per person including room, all meals and the use of our facilities. Please note there will be an additional cost for those interested in hiring sports equipment.

Reading

1 Look at the photo. How do you think these people live their lives?

2 Read the first part of the article quickly to see if you are correct.

People of the sea

(1) The Mokens are a group of around 3000 people who live on **(2) the Andaman Sea** in **(3) south-east Asia**. They spend half of the year living on **(4) boats** and only live on land during the rainy season. Their boats are called Kabang and are made from **(5) a single tree**. **(6) The tree** becomes a home with a kitchen and living area.

(7) A boy from the Moken community often learns to swim before he can walk and will usually become **(8) a fisherman**. It is a dangerous activity but they are skilled at what they do. The Mokens respect the sea and only catch the seafood they need, eating most of it and trading anything else at local markets for other essential food such as **(9) rice**.

3 Read the text again and answer the questions.

1 How many months do the Mokens spend at sea each year?
2 How many trees are used to make a Moken boat?
3 What job does a Moken man traditionally do?
4 What do the Mokens do with food they don't eat?

Articles

▶ **GRAMMAR** REFERENCE p.129

4 Match the rules A–I with examples 1–9 from the text.

a/an

A single countable nouns that we talk about for the first time and mention again later

B before a person/thing that is just one of many in a group

C jobs

the

D single countable nouns that we have talked about before

E uncountable nouns or plural nouns when we are talking about a specific object or group

F when there is only one of something

no article

G uncountable and abstract nouns when we talk about them in general

H plural nouns when we talk about something in general

I with most streets, towns, cities, countries, continents, language and names

LANGUAGE TIP

Knowing which nouns are countable and which are uncountable will help you to use articles correctly.

5 Turn to page 123 to keep reading *People of the sea*.

Speaking

6 Work in pairs and discuss the questions.

1 Are there any groups of people that have an unusual way of life in your country? Who?
2 Is their way of life likely to survive in future? Why/ Why not?
3 What traditions in your country do you think should be protected? Why?

Speaking

1 Work in pairs and discuss the questions.

1 Why do people use more water these days?
2 What problems does a lack of water cause?
3 Why is it so difficult to transport fresh water to places that need it?

Writing

Informal letter (Part 3)

▶ **WRITING** REFERENCE p.143

▶ **FUNCTIONS** BANK p.155

2 Work in pairs. Read the instructions and complete the prompts with three pieces of advice for Jamie.

1 You should…
2 Why don't you…
3 You could…

This is part of a letter you receive from an English friend, Jamie.

> So, the university have just had a water meter put in all the accommodation blocks, and we'll have to use less water around the flat, but I'm not really sure where to start. Do you have any ideas?

Now write a letter to Jamie about ways to use less water. Write your **letter** in about **100 words**.

---

3 Read a letter that Jamie's friend Charles wrote.

1 Does it answer the question?
2 Is it around 100 words?
3 Does it have a beginning and an ending?
4 Is it written in paragraphs?
5 Is it written in a friendly style?
6 Is it accurate?

Hi Jamie

It was great to hear from you. You'd think living on the island of Bermuda, we'd have too much water. Actually, we collect every drop we use and store it ourselves. So, here are my top tips. Don't wash the car because it's just too wasteful. Showers shorter always help. When things get really bad here, I'm even switching the water in the shower off while I shampoo my hair. I also think you should check your water system for leaks. That wastes loads off water. If you hear any other suggestions, let me know. Looking forward to hearing from you.

Take care

Charles

---

4 Divide the letter into three paragraphs (starting the letter, giving advice, ending the letter).

5 Charles wrote his answer very quickly. Look at his letter again. There are five mistakes in the answer. Can you find one example of each of the error types in the list?

1 word order
2 punctuation
3 spelling
4 preposition
5 tense

EXAM TIP

Always leave time to go back and edit your work. You are likely to lose marks if you have a lot of errors.

---

6 Now write your answer to the task. Use your ideas from Activity 2.

7 Check your own answer using the checklists in Activities 3 and 5. Can you improve your writing?

Celebrity

8

Speaking

1 **Work in pairs and discuss the questions.**

1 What job did you want to do when you were a child? Would you like to do this job now? Why/Why not?

2 What industry do most teenage girls in your country want to work in? And teenage boys? Why?

Reading

2 **Read the article about teenagers and their future careers. Is the situation similar or different to your country? Why?**

COLUMN

Teenagers aim to be stars

According to a new survey the top three industries girls would like to work in are arts and entertainment, followed by education and healthcare. The boys chose IT, followed by engineering and then arts and entertainment. So why is **show business** so attractive?

Traditionally, a famous person such as a **ballet dancer**, **stage actor** or **rock star** became well-known because they worked hard and were talented. These days celebrities aren't necessarily found working at a **film studio**, recording a **soap opera** or planning their next **stadium concert**. Instead, they might be posing for **magazine covers**, starring in **television commercials** or appearing on **chat shows**.

And unfortunately, this is what young people see – celebrities in **designer clothes** talking about their perfect lives – and are then disappointed with the reality of the working world.

Entertainment

3 **Complete the questions with the compound nouns in bold in the text.**

1 Should magazine editors only use slim models on .... ?

2 Would you prefer to be a .... in a dance company, a guitar-playing .... or a .... in the best theatres?

3 Do you think .... is a good industry to work in?

4 Would you wear .... every day if you could?

5 Would you prefer to watch a .... about a family or a .... where famous people are interviewed?

6 How do you feel about .... in the middle of your favourite programme?

7 Is there a famous .... where movies are made in your country?

8 Have you ever seen your favourite band at a .... ?

4 **Work in pairs and discuss the questions in Activity 3.**

Speaking

Extended turn (Part 3)

▶ **FUNCTIONS** BANK p.152

5 **Use the words to make sentences that are true for the photo on page 68.**

in the middle of	in front of
in the background	on the right-hand side
at the top of	on the left of	surrounding

6 **Student A, turn to page 117 and describe the photo. Student B, describe the photo on this page. Does your partner use any prepositions of place?**

General conversation (Part 4)

▶ **FUNCTIONS** BANK p.152

7 ▶ **36** **Listen to two friends, Toby and Izzy, talking about what films they like. What do they each say is their favourite?**

8 **Listen again and complete the sentences with a word that describes *likes* and *dislikes* from the recording.**

1 *I'm not* very .... *on* it.

2 Actually *I'm* .... old black and white films at the moment.

3 And *you can't* .... a good thriller.

4 I guess I *don't* .... them.

5 But I *really* .... romantic comedies.

6 I *can't* .... that kind of rubbish.

9 **Work in pairs. Use the expressions in Activity 8 in italics, including the words you wrote, to talk about your film likes and dislikes.**

10 **Work in different pairs. Talk together about the kinds of entertainment you enjoy for three to four minutes. Here are some things you could talk about.**

1 Your favourite and least favourite type of entertainment, e.g. music, films, television, gaming, the theatre.

2 The most popular kinds of entertainment in your country.

3 Why you prefer to stay in or go out.

4 Whether you would like to work in the entertainment industry, and why/why not.

Speaking

1 **Work in pairs. Look at the photo and discuss the questions.**

1 Why do you think the photographers are so interested in the woman?

2 Would you like to be famous? Why/Why not?

Reading

Multiple-choice cloze (Part 5)

2 **Read the headline of the text. Work in pairs and discuss the questions.**

1 What do you think the five most famous brands in the world are?

2 Is it possible for a person to be a brand? If yes, which famous people do you think are brands?

3 **Read the text quickly to find out if your answers to Activity 2 were correct.**

> **EXAM TIP**
>
> Make sure each option you choose fits the meaning and grammar of the sentence.

4 **Read the text again and choose the correct word for each space. Mark the correct letter A–D.**

0 A round	**B over**	C close	D hardly
1 **A** either	B none	**C** neither	D nothing
2 A front	B case	C order	**D** fact
3 **A** whose	B which	C whom	D where
4 **A** spends	B takes	C gives	D brings
5 A with	B in	**C** for	D at
6 A true	B natural	C acceptable	**D** honest
7 A strong	B heavy	C serious	**D** strict
8 A should	B was	**C** would	D had
9 A make	**B** get	C receive	D gain
10 **A** adverts	B writing	C newspapers	D articles

5 **Work in pairs and discuss why the words you have NOT chosen do not fit spaces 1–3 in Activity 4.**

Speaking

6 **Work in pairs. What are the positives and negatives of fame for celebrities like Kim Kardashian?**

The woman whose life is a brand

Kim Kardashian has **(0)** ..over........... five million Twitter followers but she's **(1)** .... a singer nor an actor. In **(2)** ...., she's a reality TV star **(3)** .... programme is seen by millions. She's **surprised** by her fame but explains that the world is **fascinated** by other people's lives.

Kim **(4)** .... her time selling her **interesting** life like a product **(5)** .... everyone to see. She says that if she had a great voice it would be **amazing** but she's **(6)** .... and knows that her talent is marketing herself. Kim's childhood taught her about hard work. Her father was **(7)** .... with her and **(8)** .... not allow her to go out at night. He made her **(9)** .... a job to pay for her first car.

Kim used to find untrue magazine **(10)** .... **frightening** and **depressing** but now she isn't **worried** and is **encouraged** by her kind fans.

Vocabulary

-ed and -ing adjectives

7 **Match the bold adjectives in the article with the definitions 1–8.**

1 the feeling when something unexpected happens
2 describes something that keeps your attention
3 feel extremely interested
4 describes something that makes you feel sad
5 feel stress about a problem
6 given confidence
7 describes something that is very unexpected
8 describes something that makes you feel afraid

8 **Look at the adjectives and definitions in Activity 7 and answer the questions.**

What suffix is used at the end of adjectives that

1 describe a person's feelings?
2 describe the thing that causes the person's feelings?

LANGUAGE TIP

Like regular past simple verbs, the -ed at the end of adjectives can be pronounced /t/, e.g. *depressed*; /d/ e.g. *amazed*; or /ɪd/ e.g. *interested*.

9 **How are the -ed adjectives in Activity 7 pronounced?**

10 **Choose the correct adjective in each sentence.**

1 I find celebrity magazines really *depressing/amazing* and never read them.
2 People are *fascinated/interesting* by the lives that other people have.
3 I'm *frightening/worried* that celebrities are having a bad influence on young people.
4 It's *interesting/surprised* to follow celebrities on social networks.
5 I'm *frightening/surprised* that celebrities have to work hard to stay successful.
6 I'm *encouraged/depressing* by the charity work that many celebrities do.
7 It's *frightening/worried* that so many young people want to be famous.
8 Celebrities only look *amazing/fascinated* because they can afford the best clothes.

Speaking

11 **Work in groups. You are going to take part in a television debate called 'Are celebrities good role models for young people?' Use the ideas in Activity 10 to help you prepare.**

12 **Role-play the television debate.**

Student A: You are the TV presenter of the debate show. Prepare questions to ask your guests about their opinions.

Student B: You are a celebrity. You think the answer to the question is *yes*.

Student C: You are a secondary school student. You think the answer to the question is *yes*.

Student D: You are a parent. You think the answer to the question is *no*.

Student E: You are a university student. You think the answer to the question is *no*.

Reported speech

▶ **GRAMMAR** REFERENCE p.129

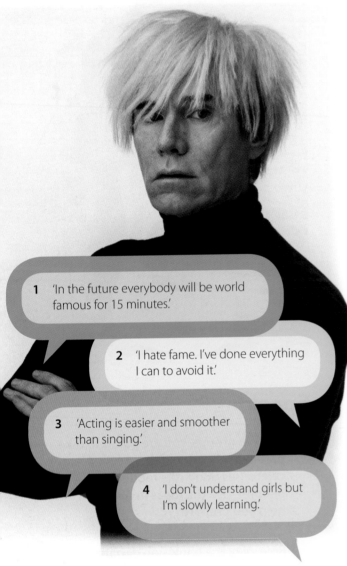

1 'In the future everybody will be world famous for 15 minutes.'

2 'I hate fame. I've done everything I can to avoid it.'

3 'Acting is easier and smoother than singing.'

4 'I don't understand girls but I'm slowly learning.'

1 Work in pairs and look at quote 1. Do you think the prediction has come true? Why/Why not?

2 Quotes 1–4 are from four famous people. Which speaker

A doesn't like life in the public eye?

B doesn't always know what women are thinking?

C is comparing one thing to another?

D is making a prediction?

3 Can you complete the sentences with a name from the box?

| Johnny Depp | Beyoncé Knowles |
| Daniel Radcliffe | Andy Warhol |

1 .... said that everybody *would be* world-famous for fifteen minutes in the future.

2 .... said that he *hated* fame and *had done* everything he *could* to avoid it.

3 .... said that acting *was* easier and smoother than singing.

4 .... said he *didn't understand* girls but *was* slowly *learning*.

4 Use quotes 1–4 and the sentences in Activity 3 to complete the table.

direct speech	reported speech
present simple	
present continuous	
past simple	past perfect
present perfect simple	
will	
can	*could*

5 Complete the second sentence in each pair so it means the same as the first. Use between one and three words.

1 *Lady Gaga:* 'I don't like celebrities. I don't hang out with them.'

Lady Gaga said she didn't like celebrities and .... with them.

2 *Will Ferrell:* 'I have only been funny about seventy-four percent of the time.'

Will Ferrell said he .... funny about seventy-four percent of the time.

3 *Maria Sharapova:* 'I am beautiful, famous and gorgeous.'

Maria Sharapova said .... beautiful, famous and gorgeous.

4 *David Beckham:* 'I always wanted to be a hairdresser.'

David Beckham said he .... to be a hairdresser.

5 *Robert Downey Jr:* 'I'm thinking of getting a monkey.'

Robert Downey Jr said .... of getting a monkey.

6 Work in pairs. Are any of the quotes in Activity 5 surprising? Why/Why not?

LANGUAGE TIP

Say does not need an object but *tell* does, e.g. *He **said** he didn't live around here. She **told me** we'd met before.*

7 Work in pairs. Student A turn to page 115. Student B turn to page 116. Follow the instructions.

Speaking

1 Look at the advert for the New York Reality TV school. Work in pairs and discuss the questions.

1 Would you be interested in this school? Why/Why not?

2 What reality TV shows are popular in your country?

3 Why do people want to watch or appear on reality TV shows?

The New York
Reality TV School

We'll help you become confident and get you ready for the world of Reality TV. We can help you be selected by producers and win the big prizes! What are you waiting for?

→ **CLICK** to find out more.

Listening
Gap-fill (Part 3)

2 ▶ 37 Listen to Michelle Washington, a teacher at the New York Reality TV School, talking about appearing on reality TV. Choose the best word to complete the gap.

1 Michelle thinks you should talk to your .... before applying for a reality TV show.

3 Listen again and answer the questions.

1 In Activity 2, how many words for 'people' did you hear?

2 What helped you decide which word was the correct answer?

EXAM TIP

You may hear several words that could fit the gap, but only one choice will be correct.

4 You will hear Michelle Washington talking to a group of students about courses at the New York Reality TV School. Read through the notes and predict what kind of information you are listening for.

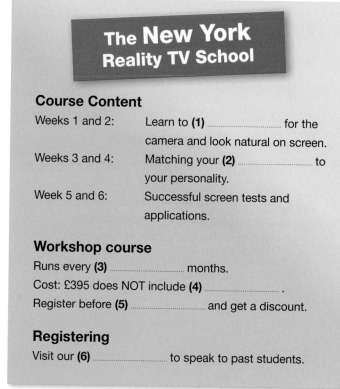

The New York
Reality TV School

Course Content

Weeks 1 and 2:   Learn to **(1)** .... for the camera and look natural on screen.

Weeks 3 and 4:   Matching your **(2)** .... to your personality.

Week 5 and 6:   Successful screen tests and applications.

Workshop course

Runs every **(3)** .... months.

Cost: £395 does NOT include **(4)** ....

Register before **(5)** .... and get a discount.

Registering

Visit our **(6)** .... to speak to past students.

5 ▶ 38 Listen and fill in the missing information in the numbered spaces 1–6.

Speaking

6 Work in pairs and discuss the questions.

1 Would you like someone to advise you on how to dress and present yourself? Why/Why not?

2 What qualities does someone need to be a star?

Speaking

1 Work in pairs and discuss the questions.

1 What types of workers do celebrities employ?

2 Would you want the girl in the photo working as your personal assistant? Why/Why not?

Listening

2 ▶ 39 You will hear a girl named Honey being interviewed for a job as a personal assistant for a celebrity. Do you think she will get the job? Why/Why not?

3 Listen again and complete the questions.

1 .... ever worked as a personal assistant before?

2 .... you able to work days, nights and weekends?

3 .... any questions for me?

4 .... I meet?

5 .... I start?

Reported questions

▶ **GRAMMAR** REFERENCE p.130

4 ▶ 40 Listen to Honey telling her friend about the experience. Complete the sentences with the words Honey uses.

1 They asked me .... ever worked as a personal assistant before.

2 They asked me .... able to work nights and weekends.

3 She asked me .... questions ....

4 I asked .... meet.

5 I asked .... start!

5 Look at questions 1–5 in Activities 3 and 4 again.

1 Underline the main verbs.

2 How does the word order change when we report questions?

3 What word do we add when we report yes/no questions?

6 Look at the dictionary entry. Have you ever been to an audition for anything? How did (or would) you feel?

> **Audition** /ɔːˈdɪʃən $ ɒː-/ n [C] a short recording by an actor, singer etc. to test whether he or she is good enough to perform in a play, concert, etc.

7 Some young actors are asking a film director questions about auditions. Look at the questions and complete the second sentence in each pair so that it has a similar meaning to the first.

1 'Is it important to learn all the words?' one actor from New York asked.

He asked .... to learn all the words.

2 'My director asked, "Do you have any questions?"' says Suzie from Ohio. 'What was he expecting?'

Suzie's director asked .... any questions. Suzie wanted to know what ....

3 'How should I prepare for the audition?' That question is from Jack in Florida.

Jack asked .... prepare for the audition.

4 'Will it be okay to look straight at the camera?' Jennifer from LA asks.

Jennifer asked .... okay to look straight at the camera.

5 Melanie from Texas asks, 'What's the best thing to say at the end of the audition?'

Melanie asked .... to say at the end of the audition.

> **LANGUAGE TIP**
>
> Direct speech is common in stories, but reported speech is more common in most other situations.

8 ▶ 41 Listen to the director's answers. What advice does he give?

9 Work in pairs. Student A, turn to page 115. Student B, turn to page 116. Follow the instructions.

10 Work in new pairs. Who can remember the most questions they asked and the answers they received in Activity 9?

Writing
Story (Part 3)

▶**WRITING** REFERENCE p.145

1 **Work in pairs and discuss the questions.**

1 When can ordinary people appear on television?
2 Do you know anyone who's appeared on television or in the news? What for?
3 Would you like to be on television? On what kind of programme?

2 **Look at the exam task below. Do you have any experiences that could help you write the story?**

> Your English teacher has asked you to write a story.
> Your story must have the following title:
> *I was nearly famous*
> Write your **story** in about **100 words**.

3 **Work in pairs. Look at the sentences from a student's answer. Put sentences A–G in the correct order.**

1 I was nearly famous …
2 ....
3 ....
4 ....
5 ....
6 ....
7 ....
8 ....
9 But I was nearly famous!

4 **Divide the story in Activity 3 into paragraphs.**

EXAM TIP

It is important that your story has a clear beginning, middle and end.

5 **Write your own answer to the exam task in Activity 2.**

6 **When you have finished, swap stories with a partner and check that they have**

1 set the scene, included main events and written a good ending.
2 divided your story into paragraphs.
3 added some dialogue to make the story exciting.
4 used adjectives, adverbs and linking words.

A One winter, my friend and I were travelling in the mountains when suddenly the car stopped.

B She was just about to interview me for the TV show *Famous Rescues*, when they received a phone call.

C Hours later, when I got to the bottom, a van appeared and a well-known news presenter got out and asked what'd happened.

D 'We're going to die here!' my friend cried; I wasn't worried because I knew there was a town at the bottom of the mountain, so I set off for help.

E 'What a brave guy!' she said, after hearing my story, and ordered the camera crew to get their cameras ready.

F I tried to re-start it, but it didn't move.

G The presenter explained that a film star had just arrived, and they had to film her instead.

PROGRESS TEST 4

1 **Complete the text on bottled water with _a_ / _an_ / _the_ or (–) if you think that no article is necessary.**

The price of water

These days around the world, we spend over $50 billion on bottled water each year. Before 1995, **(1)** .... bottled water industry hardly existed. Many people disagree with bottling water, despite **(2)** .... fact that it's clearly popular. There's **(3)** .... strong environmental argument against the industry, which creates at least 200 million plastic bottles around **(4)** .... world each year. Less than **(5)** .... quarter of those bottles ever reaches **(6)** .... recycling. Secondly, in many countries, such as **(7)** .... United States or Britain, water from taps is safe to drink and costs around one cent per litre, so bottled water is a very expensive alternative. Although some bottled water comes from **(8)** .... underground sources, and may have health benefits, some just contain tap water. Finally, there are also concerns that selling water isn't morally correct. Water, like **(9)** .... air, is one of the absolute basics of life, and nobody would think of putting **(10)** .... price on that.

2 **Put the words in the correct place in the table, then add one more example of each.**

abstract nouns   activities   animals
gases   jobs   languages   ~~liquids~~
materials   objects   ~~people~~   plants
units of measurement

Countable nouns		
1 _people_	**1**	mate
2	**2**	rose
3	**3**	giraffe
4	**4**	dictionary
5	**5**	metre
6	**6**	waiter
Uncountable nouns		
7	**7**	wood
8 _liquids_	**8**	oil
9	**9**	air
10	**10**	surfing
11	**11**	Chinese
12	**12**	honesty

3 **Complete the sentences with the words from the list.**

blowing   cloudy   dry   frost   gales
showers   snowfall   thunderstorm
cool   wet

And now, today's weather

Weather forecasts are more accurate today than ever before. We can predict things like **(1)** .... weather from photos of rain clouds moving across the planet, and its opposite, **(2)** .... weather. Although it's easy to see rain coming, it's hard to predict exactly where short **(3)** .... will fall. Another difficult one to see coming is a **(4)** .... These noisy storms happen when **(5)** .... air above meets warmer air below. Without strong winds such as **(6)** .... to get everything moving around, you're unlikely to see violent weather.

Late for work because you have to get the ice off your car in the mornings? Well, a thick, white **(7)** .... is surprisingly hard to predict. Cold temperatures are necessary, but if there's a wind **(8)** .... that night, there'll be no ground ice the next day. Also, if it's a **(9)** .... night, you won't need to set the alarm earlier only clear skies produce iced cars.

The hardest one to predict is **(10)** .... No single computer model can tell you if your skiing holiday will be a disappointment or not. It might be easier just to look on the internet!

4 **Complete the gaps 1–8 with the correct preposition.**

Tanzanian high school student, Erasto B Mpemba was trying to make ice-cream one day and was worried **(1)** .... the results. He did not have time to wait for his mixture to cool before freezing it. However, Mpemba's hot mixture froze faster than his classmate's cold mixture. When he told the class, they were so interested **(2)** .... his discovery that he was able to involve them all **(3)** .... an experiment to show he was right.

In fact, Aristotle, a man famous **(4)** .... teaching Alexander the Great about science, had noticed the same thing. Anyone familiar **(5)** .... chemistry will know that cold water freezes fastest, but hot water freezes at a higher temperature than cold, now called the 'Mpemba effect'. Freeze water to below 120 degrees, and you will be amazed **(6)** .... what happens–water changes from ice to a liquid similar **(7)** .... honey. Anyone keen **(8)** .... learning more, please come along to our Science in the Community Fair this weekend!

5 **Look at the passage below and choose the best word (A-D) to complete the gaps.**

Drink up!

Forget vitamin pills, water can be just as important for your health. For many years now, water's been **(1)** .... for its positive effect on appearance. In one **(2)** .... survey, scientists found that 50 percent of people looked younger after regularly drinking more water. But there are health **(3)** .... , too. If you're **(4)** .... about low energy levels, water can help you feel more awake. It also helps you get more from your **(5)** .... The body works better when you've had enough to drink. It'll also help people trying to lose a few **(6)** .... as water stops you feeling hungry. Very often people who complain of **(7)** .... might find that it's the body's way of saying that it's dried out. A study even said that drinking more water **(8)** .... help to avoid heart attacks in the future. At the very least, it'll help you to **(9)** .... on work better. So, next time you're thirsty, reach for a **(10)** .... of water, rather than the coffee.

1	A understood	B aware	C known	D seen
2	A surprising	B interested	C confusing	D fascinated
3	A advantage	B benefits	C bonus	D profit
4	A tired	B fascinating	C interested	D worried
5	A move	B workout	C exercise	D active
6	A kilos	B weight	C dress sizes	D heaviness
7	A aches	B illnesses	C headaches	D infections
8	A would	B had	C is going to	D has
9	A consider	B think	C pay attention	D concentrate
10	A jar	B mug	C cup	D glass

6 **Look at the sentences below and write them in reported speech.**

1 'This is my latest film,' Anne said.
2 'I've already written my autobiography,' Leonardo explained.
3 'I'll start my own perfume business,' said Sarah.
4 'I can act in serious plays as well!' Elle argued.
5 'I don't want to give any more interviews,' Wayne said.
6 'Our new single sold 100,000 copies last month', the band told us.

7 **Look at the report of an interview with a reality TV star called Chantelle. Write the reported speech in direct speech.**

1 I asked Chantelle if she had any plans for the next six months.
2 I asked where Chantelle had been on holiday this year.
3 I asked what Chantelle was planning to wear to the reality TV awards.
4 One of our readers asked how Chantelle usually spent her weekends.
5 I asked if Chantelle had had any plastic surgery done.
6 I asked her if she would come back and talk to us next month.

8 **Match each first half of the sentence (1–8) with the second half (A–H).**

1 Tom Hanks has worked in show
2 Natalie Portman trained to be a ballet
3 Ozzy Osbourne started his career as a rock
4 Old stars, like Marilyn Monroe, needed the support of film
5 Russell Crowe started his career in an Australian soap
6 Oprah Winfrey was one of America's top chat
7 Stella McCartney produces designer
8 Gisele Bündchen has appeared on hundreds of magazine

A opera called *Neighbours*.
B covers during her career.
C business for years.
D studios for their success.
E star before appearing in reality TV.
F show presenters.
G dancer before she filmed *Black Swan*.
H clothes for a lot of stars.

9 **Here are some sentences about where celebrities relax. Complete the second sentence so that it means the same as the first. Use no more than three words.**

1 'Where do all the celebrities go when they want to relax?' our reporter asked.
Our reporter asked where all .... when they wanted to relax.
2 Most celebrities said that the Burj Al Arab in Dubai was the most luxurious hotel they knew.
Most celebrities .... us that the Burj Al Arab in Dubai was the most luxurious hotel they knew.
3 Many said that they liked Majorca.
Many said that they .... on Majorca.
4 Most wanted any place that was relaxing.
Most wanted any place where they felt ....
5 St Tropez interested a lot of sports stars.
A lot of sports stars found St Tropez ....
6 One model said that she loved Croatia for its incredible views.
One model said, '................. Croatia for its incredible views.'

Creativity

9

Speaking

1 **Work in pairs and discuss the questions.**

1 What creative subjects did you study at school?

2 Do you think being creative and being intelligent are the same thing? Why/Why not?

3 How important is it for schools to encourage young people to be creative?

2 ▶ 42 **You will hear an education expert called Roger talking about creativity at school. What does Roger say makes it difficult to become creative? Do you agree with him?**

Extended turn (Part 3)

▶ **FUNCTIONS** BANK p.153

3 **Look at the drawing by an artist called Lee Hadwin. What do you think the artist is trying to say in the drawing?**

4 ▶ 43 **Listen to three people describing the drawing. Match the descriptions 1–3 with images from the drawing.**

5 **Listen again and complete the gaps.**

1 There's a thing that looks .... a space ship.

2 There's a sky that .... unusual, with squares.

3 In the middle there's a ball – .... it's the world.

4 There's something that .... fingers, but on the feet.

5 This is definitely .... to be a woman's foot.

EXAM TIP

If you don't know the word for something in the photographs, find a way of describing it with words you do know.

6 **Work in pairs. Turn to page 117 and look at the objects. Take turns to explain one of the objects to your partner.**

7 **Work in pairs. Turn to page 119 and complete the Speaking task.**

Reading

8 You are going to read about the artist Lee Hadwin. Look at the text quickly. What's unusual about Lee's artistic ability?

TODAY

The sleep artist

Meet Lee Hadwin, a nurse with no artistic skills at all – when he's awake. But while he's sleeping, he's **able to produce** amazing drawings.

Lee realised he **could draw** in his sleep when he was a teenager. One embarrassing morning, he woke up at a friend's house to discover he'd drawn on the kitchen walls, but he **wasn't able to remember** the experience.

Sleep experts today don't know why he **can do** this, but Lee believes that in the future they **may be able to explain** why it happens. In the meantime, he'll hopefully **be able to show** his art to the public very soon.

9 Read the text again and answer the questions.

1 How did Lee discover he had the ability to create drawings in his sleep?
2 Do doctors know why Lee draws in his sleep?
3 What is Lee planning to do with his drawings?
4 What do Lee's abilities suggest about creative skills?

Modals of ability

▶ **GRAMMAR** REFERENCE p.130

10 Complete the rules with *can*, *could* and *be able to*. Use the examples in bold in the text to help you.

1 Use .... and .... to talk about present ability.
2 Use .... to talk about abilities in the past.
3 Use .... to talk about ability on one occasion in the past.
4 Use .... after *will*, *may*, present perfect simple, etc.

11 Look at the letter and complete the gaps with *can*, *could*, *be able to* and an appropriate verb from the list.

design   not draw   hand   let   make   not use

○○○   ► Search

Dear Jen

Thanks for your letter! Yes, I **(1)** .... in my art project on time, but only just!

You know how I **(2)** .... or paint? Well, fortunately this time we had to create our project digitally. Before the project, I **(3)** .... the software at all but after a bit of practice I **(4)** .... a really good piece of art. Now I **(5)** .... all kinds of wonderful pictures!

I'll send you one and you **(6)** .... me know what you think! Anyway, speak to you soon.

Oliver

LANGUAGE TIP

Can and *could* are also used for requests. *Can I open a window? Could I borrow a pen?*

12 Work in pairs. Student A turn to page 119. Student B turn to page 120. Follow the instructions.

13 Do a survey of the students in your class using the ideas from Activity 12. Were your guesses correct?

1 Justin is a keen photographer. He'd like to exchange ideas with other photographers and learn to improve his pictures on the computer. He's not free on Wednesdays.

2 Ursula used to run her own photographic business. She wants to go on a challenging course with photographers of a similar standard where she can practise taking landscape photos during long country walks.

3 Nina knows nothing about photography. She's going away for two weeks and wants an introduction to some basic skills so she can take photos of her trips. She's free on weekday evenings.

4 Scott wants to attend daytime classes where he will learn a lot in a short time. He hopes to learn to take different types of photos and then try out his new skills.

Speaking

1 **Work in pairs and discuss the questions.**

1 How do you feel when you look at these photos?
2 Who or what do you usually take photos of?
3 Do you share your photos online? Why/Why not?

Reading

Matching (Part 2)

2 **The people on the right all want to take a photography course. On the opposite page there are descriptions of eight courses. Decide which course A–H would be suitable for the the people 1–5.**

5 Dave has done photography for many years and is thinking of starting his own business, taking pictures of people and their families and pets. He is only free at weekends.

EXAM TIP

Choose the course that matches <u>all</u> of the needs and wants in the description of the person.

Photography Courses

A Stepping Up
On this beginner course, you will learn how to take holiday photos. Lessons take place on Wednesdays from 7 to 9 p.m., with the first two in the college photography department. We will then move to other outdoor venues nearby to practise what we've learnt.

B Skills Develo p.m.ent
This is for those photographers who have already completed a course but are not content with just taking holiday pictures. We will examine different types of professional photos and artistic techniques. Lessons are on Tuesdays from 6 and 8 p.m..

C At the Top
This Wednesday course, from 6 to 9 p.m., is for experienced photographers who would like to become more creative. We will look at how to take artistic pictures in a studio and outside. We will study photographs by famous photographers and experiment with the techniques they used.

D Wildlife
Whether you are going on a trip to Kenya or to the local river, taking photos of wildlife is never easy. This is an ideal course for photographers who have never had any formal training and would like to get some practical help. Lessons are on Saturdays from 2 to 4 p.m..

E Multi-skills
No experience is necessary for this course which provides you with forty hours of study. You will be shown how to take photos of people, places and objects. The second week will be in various locations so you can practise what you have learnt. The lessons are from Monday to Friday, 9 a.m. to 1 p.m..

F Digital skills
This Thursday course, 8 to 10 p.m., is for all levels. You'll learn how to use digital technology to edit your photos, for example by removing red eyes from family photos. We request you bring your own photos to classes. Classmates are encouraged to share their knowledge with each other.

G Portraits
This Saturday morning course is for photographers who already have considerable experience. It will be in our photography studio so we can teach you how to take pictures of people to a professional standard. Advice will also be given on earning money from your camera skills.

H On the Go
This course is for experienced photographers interested in taking better photos of the world around us. Each Wednesday we will depart for the countryside at 9 a.m. so you can develop your camera skills further. However, you must be prepared to spend all day on your feet as we don't return until 5 p.m..

Redlake COLLEGE

Vocabulary
Formal language

> **LANGUAGE TIP**
>
> When you learn a new word, use a dictionary to find out if it is used in formal or informal situations.

> **depart** /dɪˈpɑːt $ -ɑːt/dv [I] *formal* to leave:
> [+from] *The train will depart from Platform 4.*
> [+for] *He departed for Rome immediately.*

3 **Match the words below with a more formal synonym from the texts.**

1 finished (text B)
2 want (text C)
3 gives (text E)
4 ask for (text F)
5 leave (text H)
6 more (text H)

4 **Make the sentences below more formal.**

1 If you want more information, please email us.
2 We give you advice about taking holiday photos before you leave for the airport.
3 You can ask for a certificate when you finish the course.

Speaking

5 **Work in pairs and discuss the questions.**

1 Which of the courses would you most like to do?
2 Think of a photo that's special to you. What does it show? Why is it special? Where do you keep it?

Writing

6 **Imagine you've received an email from an English friend. Read part of the email and then write a reply, answering the questions.**

So, anyway I still can't believe my photo won first prize in the competition but I'm not complaining! I was so happy. Are you good with a camera? What's the best photo you've ever taken?

Speaking

1 Work in pairs and discuss the questions.

1 Do you enjoy playing online video games? Why/Why not?

2 Do you think that playing online games is a good use of people's time? Why/Why not?

3 Look at the photograph of a gamer. How is he feeling?

2 ▶ 44 **You will hear a man called Tom talking about his work on the effects of playing online games. Listen to Tom introducing his ideas.**

1 What does he think about people who play online games?

A They should spend more time playing.

B The amount of time they spend playing is okay.

C They should spend less time playing.

3 Work in small groups. Why do you think Tom has this opinion about online games? Think of at least five reasons.

EXAM TIP

Try not to guess answers from your knowledge of things in the past. Answers can be surprising.

Listening
Multiple choice (Part 2)

4 **You will hear the rest of the interview with Tom. First read the questions and underline the key words.**

1 Tom realised online games could have other uses when he

A saw gamers doing important work.

B tried new games as part of his studies.

C heard someone give a talk on gaming.

2 Tom says people enjoy online games because

A the level of difficulty is controlled.

B the players know it's not real.

C the aims are clear.

3 Tom thinks the main skill gamers learn is

A using the internet well.

B finding answers to problems.

C communicating with others.

4 What makes the online game 'World of Warcraft' so popular?

A its artwork

B its characters

C its help system

5 Tom says the people he worked with saw the benefits of gaming after they

A heard about an ancient game.

B looked at some test results.

C played a fun game together.

6 Tom's next project will ask gamers to work on the problem of

A health.

B being poor.

C the environment.

5 ▶ 45 Listen and answer questions 1–6 in Activity 3, choosing the best answers A–C.

Speaking

6 Work in pairs and discuss the questions.

1 Do you agree with Tom's idea that games teach positive skills? Why/Why not?

2 Would you be interested in the projects Tom describes? Why/Why not?

Speaking

1 Work in pairs and discuss the questions.

1 Have you ever played games like the ones in the pictures? What did you think of them?

2 Which games aren't interesting for you? Why?

2 Look at some descriptions of the games in the pictures. Which one is being described in each?

1 The people *that you create* are surprisingly realistic.

2 It's an enjoyable game *that sports fans will love.*

3 The gamer controls a group of people *who find themselves in everyday situations.*

4 You can manage players *whose skills are poor* and turn them into the best.

5 Santiago Bernebeu, *where Real Madrid play*, is just one of the stadiums you can compete in.

6 Everyone has their own personality characteristics, *which you give them*, so they don't always get along!

Relative clauses

▶ **GRAMMAR** REFERENCE p.130

3 Look at the relative clauses in *italics* in Activity 2, and answer the questions.

1 Which relative clauses are necessary to define or identify the noun (defining relative clauses)?

2 Which relative clauses give extra information about the noun (non-defining relative clauses)?

3 What are the differences in punctuation between defining and non-defining relative clauses?

4 In which sentences could you use the word *that*?

LANGUAGE TIP

We don't use *that* in non-defining clauses. *Tetris, ~~that~~ which is still played today, was created in 1984.*

4 Look at the pairs of sentences. Join the sentences using a defining relative clause.

1 In the 1980s, Alexey Pajitnov created a computer game. He called it *Tetris*.

2 Albert Einstein developed a theory of energy. He called it the theory of relativity.

3 Walt Disney created the modern idea of theme parks. People can spend the whole day there.

4 Leonardo Da Vinci was an artist and engineer. His helicopter design became a reality centuries later.

5 Add the extra information in brackets to each sentence using a non-defining relative clause.

0 *Shakespeare wrote almost 40 plays. (He was born in 1564.)*
Shakespeare, who was born in 1564, wrote almost 40 plays.

1 Marie Curie is famous for researching radioactivity and developing modern medicine. (She won two Nobel prizes.)

2 Thomas Midgely has been described as the most dangerous man that ever lived. (His inventions included putting lead into petrol and CFC gases.)

3 JK Rowling wrote the *Harry Potter* books and sold over 400 million copies. (The books encouraged millions of children to read.)

4 Steve Jobs created many modern technological inventions including the iPad. (He was Chief Executive of Apple.)

Speaking

6 Work in pairs. Which people in Activities 4 and 5 do you think have had the most influence on the world? Number them 1–9 (1 for most influence and 9 for least influence).

Speaking

1 **Work in pairs and discuss the questions.**

1 What job do you do or would like to do in future? Describe what it involves.

2 Would you like to do the job in the photo? Why/Why not?

Job skills

2 ▶ **46** **Listen to three people describing their jobs to a group of teenagers. What do you think each person's job is?**

3 **Listen again. Which speaker (1, 2 or 3) has to have each skill?**

A   be good with numbers

B   have leadership skills

C   be computer-literate

D   be good at working in a team

E   have problem-solving skills

F   have good communication skills

G   pay attention to detail

H   be organised

4 **Work in pairs and discuss the questions.**

1 Think of two more jobs that need skills A–H from Activity 3.

2 What skills do you need for your job or the job you'll do in the future?

Prefixes

LANGUAGE TIP

Prefixes don't change the stress of a word.

5 **Look at the sentences from the listening text and decide how the underlined prefixes change the meanings of the words in *italics*.**

1 I create or <u>re</u>*build* web pages.

2 It becomes <u>im</u>*possible* to do the job well.

3 People sometimes think my job's <u>un</u>*interesting*.

4 We <u>dis</u>*agree* with each other sometimes.

5 I have to be <u>self</u>-*confident*.

6 I have to work <u>ir</u>*regular* hours.

6 **Work in pairs. Student A, add the correct prefixes to the words in *italics*. Student B, turn to page 120.**

1 Do people think you're an ....*patient* person?

2 Is there a lot of ....*employment* in your country?

3 What job do you think you would ....*like* doing the most?

4 Would you mind working ....*regular* hours such as nights or weekends?

5 Are you the kind of person who ....*views* their work all the time?

6 Could you do an ....*interesting* job for a long time if you got a high salary?

7 Would you like to be ....-*employed* one day so you can manage yourself?

7 **Ask your partner the questions from Activity 6. Are you surprised by any of his/her answers?**

Speaking

1 **Work in pairs and discuss the questions.**

1 What song do you like at the moment?

2 What song has happy memories for you? Why?

2 **Choose the correct spelling to complete each sentence.**

1 I *beleive/believe* that a lot of music played on the radio is awful.

2 I've tried *writing/writting* my own music.

3 I sometimes borrow music from my local public *libary/library*.

4 My *naybour/neighbour* sometimes plays really loud music.

5 I like eating in *restaraunts/restaurants* with bands that play live music.

6 My friends and I made a music video, *which/wich* we posted online.

3 **Work in pairs. Are the sentences in Activity 2 true for you?**

Writing

Sentence transformations (Part 1)

4 **Choose the correct word to complete the second sentence in each pair.**

1 'Did you enjoy the concert?' asked Cameron.
Cameron asked *weather/whether* I'd enjoyed the concert.

2 The band's new album is the best they've made.
The band's new album is better than *their/there* previous ones.

3 The singer got flowers from her fans.
Fans *threw/through* flowers to the singer.

> ### EXAM TIP
>
> In this part of the exam, you must spell words correctly or you won't get the mark.

5 **Here are some sentences about how much it costs for a famous singer to record a hit song. Complete the second sentence so that it means the same as the first. Use no more than three words.**

0 *It takes a lot of money to make a hit song.*
...*Making*... *a hit song takes a lot of money.*

1 The amount of work that's involved is surprising.
I'm .... the amount of work that's involved.

2 First, the record company hires people to write the music.
First, people .... by the record company to write the music.

3 Some singers won't sing without certain items in the studio.
Some singers won't sing unless there .... certain items in the studio.

4 Advertising the song is the biggest cost.
Advertising the song costs .... money than making it.

5 It costs over a million dollars, although the song still might not be a hit.
Despite .... over a million dollars, the song still might not be a hit.

6 **Work in pairs. Look at your answers in Activity 5. Have you spelled the words correctly?**

Speaking

7 **Work in pairs and discuss the questions.**

1 What benefits does music bring to people?

2 Is it worth spending over a million dollars on making a song? Why/Why not?

What's it worth?

10

Speaking

1 **Work in pairs and discuss the questions.**

1 What kind of modern objects do you think will be valuable in the future?

2 Have you ever bought anything at an auction or online auction? Why/Why not?

Listening
Gap-fill (Part 3)

2 ▶ 47 **You will hear a man called Robbie talking with a woman called Jennifer about some items which they have received for their charity auction. Listen and complete the notes.**

1 First item: Poster by man called ....

2 Second item: Flight tickets to New York – contact Tony@ .... .org

3 ▶ 48 **You are going to hear Robbie giving information about the charity auction. Listen and complete the gaps with one or two words.**

Charity Auction Evening

Location:	(1) .... Hotel
Please contact:	Miss (2) .... if you have items for the auction
Aims:	to raise money to build a new (3) .... for homeless people

People should bring the Charity's (4) .... on the day.
Tickets for the (5) .... are expected to be the most popular item. Helpers needed for the (6) ....

EXAM TIP

If you have to write a name, pay attention to the spelling or listen for recognisable words (*High* Street, *Forest* Hotel).

Reading

4 You are going to read an article about some unusual things sold on the internet. Look at the text quickly. What do you think is the most unusual thing?

Video & Audio | Magazine | Editor's Blog | In Pictures

Crazy things sold on the internet

Think it's hard to make money selling things on the internet? Think again! You'll be surprised at some of the things that have been sold.

The contents of a whale's stomach
The contents of a whale's stomach sounds horrible but the hard rocks that ¹**are coughed** up by whales contain a rare mineral called Ambergris. Ambergris ²**has been used** in the perfume industry for centuries. A 15 kg piece which ³**was found** on a beach raised $300,000 Australian dollars in an online sale.

A cornflake shaped like the state of Illinois.
Two sisters from Virginia were surprised when they found a cornflake which they thought looked just like the state of Illinois in the USA. Although the cornflake ⁴**had been valued** at $1 at the start of the auction, it ⁵**was** eventually **bought** for a huge $1,350.

ILLINOIS

Justin Timberlake's half-eaten French toast
A piece of French toast that ⁶**had been bitten** into sold for $1,025 US dollars. The half-eaten meal was left behind in a café by singer and actor Justin Timberlake. Hundreds of people were attracted to the sale.

5 Read the article again. Match an object from the article, with the reason (A–C) why it attracted high offers.

A It reminded the seller of something else.

B It'd been touched by someone famous.

C It can be used in business.

6 Work in pairs and discuss the questions.

1 Why do you think the objects were bought?

2 What kind of person would want to buy them?

Passive voice

▶ **GRAMMAR** REFERENCE p.131

7 Look at the bold verbs 1–6 in the text and answer the questions for each one.

1 Do we know who does or did each action?

2 In each sentence, is the focus on the action or the person who did the action?

8 What verb forms are used in examples 1–6?

LANGUAGE TIP

Use '*by* + subject' when you want to stress the name of the person. *The French toast had been bitten **by** Justin Timberlake.*

9 Complete the rules with a phrase from the list.

who did it	past participle	*be*

We form the passive with the verb **(1)** be...... in any tense, and the **(2)** past participle
We use the passive voice when the action is more important than **(3)** who did it when we don't know.

10 Complete the sentences with the correct passive form of the verb in brackets.

1 The world's largest online auction site, eBay, was started Pierre Morad Omidyar. (*start*)

2 The first item which was sold was a broken laser pointer. (*sell*)

3 It was bought a collector of broken laser pointers. (*buy*)

4 The site .... by millions of people since it started. (*use*)

5 Over $7 billion is spent on the site each year. (*spend*)

6 Easier ways of sharing information about products .... in the future. (*introduce*)

11 Put the sentences into the passive voice.

1 People view over a billion eBay pages each day.

2 Somebody buys a mobile phone every six minutes on eBay.

3 In the next hour, eBay will sell 30 bikes.

4 In 2010, eBay employed more people than any other company, except Walmart.

5 Somebody was advertising a Lotus sports car for a Buy It Now price of 50p.

6 The most expensive item sold on eBay was a Lamborghini Spyder car, which somebody bought for $139,000.

12 Work in pairs and decide if the sentences in Activity 11 are true or false. Check your answers on page 121.

Speaking

1 **Work in pairs and discuss the questions.**

1 What kind of shops and services do you have in your neighbourhood? What shops or services would you like to have?

2 Do you prefer to use local independent shops or large shopping centres? Why?

Shops and services

2 **Match sentences 1–8 to the shops and services in the box.**

art gallery	beauty salon	chemist's
dry cleaner's	hairdresser's	
post office	restaurant	spa

1 'We're *offering a* ten percent *discount* on all spray tans today.'

2 'I'm here to *pick up* my clothes. Are they ready?'

3 'Can I *make an appointment* for a cut and blow-dry, please?'

4 'I'd like to *send a parcel* by airmail.'

5 'We're *giving away* throat sweets *free* with all cough medicine sold.'

6 'Could we *pay the bill*, please? We had the fish.'

7 'We *charge* £3 for entry to the sculpture exhibition.'

8 'Customers must *pay a* small *deposit* to borrow towels.'

LANGUAGE TIP

In the UK, people usually use the word *chemist's* to describe a shop where you buy medicine and beauty products. In the USA, people use the word *pharmacy*.

3 **Work in pairs and discuss the questions.**

1 Which of the shops and services in Activity 2 do you regularly use?

2 Which do you hardly ever use? Why?

4 **Complete the questions in the quiz. Use the phrases in *italics* in Activity 2 to help you.**

5 **Work in pairs. Take turns to ask and answer the questions in the quiz. Do you and your partner have similar spending habits?**

What kind of spender are you?

Do you love spending money? Are you always on the hunt for a bargain? Do you prefer to keep your money in the bank?

Answer our questions to find out!

1 How often do you .... the bill when you eat out with friends?

2 Do you prefer to .... a card or call someone on their birthday?

3 How often do you .... an appointment at the hairdresser's or beauty salon?

4 How do you feel about restaurants that .... ten percent extra for service?

5 Have you ever bought an item because the shop was .... something free with it?

6 Do you .... a takeaway yourself or pay someone else to deliver it?

7 Would you .... a deposit to reserve something you might not buy?

8 Do you visit particular shops or websites because they regularly .... discounts?

Speaking

1 Work in pairs and discuss the questions.

1 Do you think it's worth spending a lot of money on your appearance?

2 Do you think men or women spend longer getting ready to go out?

Reading

2 Read the article about British men and women. Is the situation the same in your country? Why/Why not?

METRONEWS

Men now spend longer getting ready to go out than women

It may come as something of a surprise, but it seems men are spending longer getting ready to go out than women. According to a survey of 3,000 Britons, men spend 83 minutes a day on personal grooming compared to women who take 79 minutes. Men also spend just 19p less a month on beauty products than women.

It seems as if male celebrities such as Cristiano Ronaldo and Zac Efron, who regularly ¹**get their hair styled** and ²**have designer clothes made** for them, have made it acceptable for boys and men to take more care over their appearance. As well as this, it appears that more men are ³**getting their backs waxed** and ⁴**having their nails done** by a professional at a beauty salon.

3 Read the article again and answer the questions.

1 How long do British men and British women spend getting ready?

2 How much more do British women spend on beauty products than men?

3 What beauty activities are British men doing more often these days?

4 Work in pairs and discuss the questions.

1 Is it a good thing that men are spending more time on their appearance? Why/Why not?

2 What kind of things do you or the men you know do to look good?

get/have something done

▶ **GRAMMAR** REFERENCE p.131

5 Look at the bold expressions 1–4 in the text and answer the questions.

1 Who does each action, the men, or someone else?

2 Is the person who does the action a professional? Is he/she paid money to do it?

3 How is this structure formed?
.... or .... + object + past participle

LANGUAGE TIP

Be careful with word order. *I had serviced my car* (past perfect). *I had my car serviced* (have something done).

6 Look at Dylan's diary. It's now 10.30 a.m. on Tuesday. Write the answers to the questions.

1 What did Dylan have done yesterday?

2 What's Dylan having done right now?

3 What's Dylan going to have done tomorrow?

4 What does Dylan have done every evening?

MONDAY FEBRUARY

11 a.m.: hairdresser's – hair cut

2 p.m.: eye test

4 p.m.: man – fix heating

7 p.m.: takeaway delivery

TUESDAY

9.45 a.m.: garage – repair car

10.00 a.m.: tailor – make new suit

10.15 a.m.: spa – nails

7 p.m.: takeaway delivery

WEDNESDAY

10.45 a.m.: gardener – cut grass

3.30 p.m.: cleaning company – carpets

7 p.m.: takeaway delivery

Speaking

7 Work in pairs and discuss the questions.

1 Which of the actions in Activity 5 do you have done?

2 How often do you have them done?

Speaking

1 **Work in pairs and discuss the statements. Do you agree? Why/Why not?**

1 Sales are a way of getting people to spend more money rather than less.

2 Special offers at the supermarket result in wasted food.

3 It's not enjoyable to shop with lots of other people in the sales.

4 Online shopping is much simpler.

Listening

2 ▶ **49** **Listen to two people talking about sales. Do the opinions in Activity 1 belong to Monica or Oliver?**

Reading
Multiple choice (Part 1)

3 **Look at the text. Is it an email, a note, a sign, a label or a text message? Where would you find it? What's the main message in the text?**

SALE Two for the price of one on DVDs bought in our shop today.

CHOOSE FROM OUR HUGE RANGE INSIDE.

4 **Read statements A–C. Choose the option that matches what the text in Activity 3 says.**

A You get double the number of any product you buy in the shop.

B If you buy one DVD today, you can get another one for free.

C Buy one DVD today and pay half the price you normally pay.

EXAM TIP

Read the texts before you read the three choices. Think about where you would find the text and what the main message is.

5 **Look at the text in each question on the exam paper. What does it say? Choose the correct option A–C.**

1

Joshua,
I've just heard about the new café in Elm Street. If you're planning on going to town tomorrow, why don't you try it out and let me know what it's like?
Ella

A Ella is telling Joshua about a new café she has recently been to.

B Ella suggests Joshua tries a new café and then tells her about it.

C Ella wants Joshua to go to a new café in town with her tomorrow.

2

DISABLED ACCESS TO THE SECOND FLOOR IS CURRENTLY UNAVAILABLE. WE APOLOGISE FOR ANY PROBLEMS THIS CAUSES OUR CUSTOMERS.

A Disabled customers are able to use the second floor only.

B None of the store's customers have access to the second floor.

C Wheelchair users cannot enter the second floor at the moment.

3

> Dad, there's something wrong with my new webcam. Can you take it back to the shop and ask for a refund? It's on the stairs with the receipt.

Send

The girl wants her dad

(A) to return the webcam and get her money back.

B to exchange the webcam for a new one that works.

C to lend her money so she can buy a new webcam.

4

Looking for a haircut?

Existing customers who book before Friday get a 20 percent discount.

 A Anyone can get a discount on a haircut if they book by Friday.

B Customers who have an appointment on Friday pay 20 percent less.

C Only people who've been to the shop before get a lower price.

5

> Please try on all sale items before buying them as they are non-returnable.

(A) Make sure any sale goods you buy fit you before you buy them.

B You can return any items you buy in the sale at a later date. ✗

C Because there's a sale, it's not a good idea to try clothes on.

Vocabulary
Verbs and prepositions

6 Complete the statements with a preposition. Use the texts in Activities 4 and 5 to help you.

1 I've just *heard* .... a new clothes shop that's opening.

2 I'm *looking* .... a top to go with my new trousers.

3 The shop assistant *apologised* .... giving the wrong change.

4 Josie's *planning* .... going shopping this weekend.

5 The customer *asked* the shop assistant .... help.

6 Customers can *choose* .... our large variety of science fiction books.

7 Complete the questions below with prepositions from the list.

about	for	from	in
on	to (×2)	with	

1 When was the last time you *complained* .... something in a shop?

2 How long do you spend *searching* .... a particular item of clothing that you want?

3 Whose shopping advice do you *listen* .... ?

4 Do you *insist* .... trying on all clothes before you buy them?

5 Do you usually *succeed* .... getting a bargain when you go shopping?

6 On shopping trips, which friend or family member do you sometimes *argue* .... ?

7 Have you ever *lent* money .... someone so he/she can buy something?

8 What was the last shop you *bought* something .... ?

8 ▶ 50 Listen to the questions from Activity 7. How is each preposition pronounced?

LANGUAGE TIP

Some prepositions (e.g. *at, for, from, of, to*) are usually pronounced in their weak form. However, if they come at the end of a sentence, they are pronounced in their strong form.

9 Work in pairs. Discuss the questions in Activity 7 to find out if you have similar shopping habits.

Listening

1 **Work in pairs and discuss the questions.**

1 When do people give gifts in your country?

2 What was the last gift you received?

3 Do you enjoy giving gifts to other people? Why/Why not?

2 **Look at the advertisement.**

1 Would you use a service like this?

2 Who do you find it most difficult to buy gifts for? Why?

3 ▶ 51 **You will hear a radio interview with Dan Jameson, who runs the Top Gifts, giving advice on gift-giving. Listen and answer the questions.**

1 What two things does Dan say you should consider when choosing a gift?

2 What's Dan's advice about deciding how much to spend?

4 **Listen again. Who says these phrases? Dan or the Presenter?**

1 That's a good idea, but…

2 Hmm, I'm not sure that's the best choice.

3 That might not work for me.

4 Good point.

5 That'd work!

6 Well, I couldn't agree more with that one!

Speaking

Simulated situation (Part 2)

▶ **FUNCTIONS** BANK p.153

5 **Which phrases from Activity 4 are used to agree or disagree?**

EXAM TIP

Don't use the time your partner is speaking to plan what you want to say next. You must comment on their ideas and clearly say if you agree with them.

6 **Work in pairs and discuss the questions.**

1 Do you agree with Dan's advice?

2 What's the best gift you've ever received? What made it special?

3 Do you think it's always important to spend money on a gift?

7 ▶ 52 **You will hear a boy called Josh and a girl called Bella discussing a gift for a wedding.**

1 What do they decide to buy?

2 Why do they choose not to buy the other two suggestions?

8 **Turn to page 121. Work in pairs and follow the instructions.**

Speaking

1 **Work in pairs and discuss the questions.**

1 Have you ever lost anything valuable? What? How did you feel?

2 Are you generally careful with your valuables?

3 What do you think was lost in the photograph below?

2 ▶ **53 You are going to hear a man called James talking about the most expensive items ever lost. Which item do you find the most surprising?**

3 **Listen again and decide if the sentences are true or false.**

1 The Renoir and Van Gogh paintings were important because they were the most expensive paintings ever sold.

2 The whole Amber Room was moved to keep it safe.

3 Richard Harris couldn't find his car so he gave up looking.

4 **Look at the sentences in Activity 3 again. What linking words are being used to give a reason or result?**

Writing
Note (Part 2)

▶ **FUNCTIONS** BANK p.155

5 **Read the exam task and answer the questions.**

1 What kind of things might someone lose at a party?

2 What three things do you have to do?

> You went to a party at your English friend Bethany's house and left something behind there. Write an email to Bethany. In your email you should
> • thank her for the party.
> • describe what you left there.
> • suggest when you could collect it.
> Write **35–45 words**.

6 **Read Carla's email to Bethany. Does she link her ideas well?**

> Dear Bethany,
> Thank you for the lovely party! I lost my ring there. It was my grandmother's ring. It's very special. It's unusual. It's gold and has a large pink diamond. I'll come round your house on Tuesday evening. I'll collect the ring.
> Carla

7 **Rewrite Carla's email using the linkers from Activity 4 (*so*, *because* and *to*).**

EXAM TIP

Try to use linkers to join sentences, even in shorter pieces of writing.

8 **How could you continue the sentences below?**

1 I really enjoyed the party because…

2 I put the ring down to…

3 I'm free on Friday, so…

9 **Look at the exam task and write your answer. Make sure you cover all the information points clearly, and write in longer sentences.**

> You borrowed a book from your friend Bill and now you've lost it. Write an email to Bill. In your email you should
> • apologise for losing the book.
> • explain how you lost it.
> • offer to make the situation better.
> Write **35–45 words**.

PROGRESS TEST 5

1 Decide whether the relative clauses in these sentences are correct or incorrect. Correct the ones that are incorrect. Remember to look at punctuation too.

1 Sir Isaac Newton who was lived in the 17th century was a famous mathematician.

2 Thomas Edison was a businessman who most famous invention was the light bulb.

3 Michelangelo grew up near Florence, where he was sent to study as a boy.

4 Sigmund Freud, who was an Austrian scientist, was interested in the meaning of dreams.

5 Mozart's music, that was written over 300 years ago, is still very popular today.

6 George Washington, was the first president of the USA, only had one tooth when he got the job.

2 Complete the sentences with *can, could, be able to* (in the correct form) and a verb from the list.

come	finish	go	find	paint
play	read	see		

1 When Tristan was young, he .... three musical instruments.

2 .... you .... what that sign says over there?

3 I tried to bake you a birthday cake but I .... it in time.

4 I'm sorry but I .... for dinner next week.

5 My daughter .... landscapes well as a child.

6 Pavel has to wear glasses or he .... anything!

7 I drove around for ages before I .... a parking space.

8 Claudia's ill this morning so she .... to work.

3 Put the word in brackets in the correct form using an appropriate prefix.

1 Leo gets very .... when he has to wait. (*patient*)

2 I have to work .... hours in my job, including nights. (*regular*)

3 Cecilia doesn't have a lot of .... (*confidence*)

4 It's difficult to find a job because of the high .... in the area. (*employment*)

5 After the storm, we had to .... our chimney. (*build*)

6 I'm sorry but I .... with your opinions of the film. (*agree*)

7 My dad's a .... builder. He loves working for himself. (*employed*)

8 No-one can do this exercise. It's .... ! (*possible*)

9 Living so far from the train station is a big .... for me. (*advantage*)

10 If you're feeling .... , don't come to work. (*well*)

4 Complete the sentences with the correct preposition.

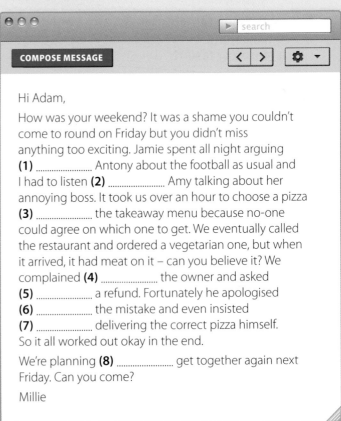

Hi Adam,

How was your weekend? It was a shame you couldn't come to round on Friday but you didn't miss anything too exciting. Jamie spent all night arguing **(1)** .... Antony about the football as usual and I had to listen **(2)** .... Amy talking about her annoying boss. It took us over an hour to choose a pizza **(3)** .... the takeaway menu because no-one could agree on which one to get. We eventually called the restaurant and ordered a vegetarian one, but when it arrived, it had meat on it – can you believe it? We complained **(4)** .... the owner and asked **(5)** .... a refund. Fortunately he apologised **(6)** .... the mistake and even insisted **(7)** .... delivering the correct pizza himself. So it all worked out okay in the end.

We're planning **(8)** .... get together again next Friday. Can you come?

Millie

5 Put the verbs in brackets in the correct passive form.

How education has changed

Before writing, history **(1)** .... (pass) on to young people through storytelling. After writing **(2)** ....(invent), it was possible to keep records of history and so more formal types of education **(3)** .... (introduce) but often only rich families could afford them.

The first university **(4)** .... (build) around a thousand years ago. However, it wasn't until the 19th century that schools **(5)** ....(provide) by governments for all children to attend. In the 21st century, most children around the world **(6)** .... (educate) at school although sadly some children **(7)** .... (still/not/give) this opportunity.

In the last two decades, education **(8)** .... (change) by new technology. Today, the internet **(9)** .... (use) in class so that students can access a lot of information. In the future, it's possible that classes **(10)** .... (attend) by students from all over the world via computer.

6 Complete the sentences with the words in brackets and *have something done* in the correct form.

1 Doesn't Saira look lovely? I think she .... yesterday. (*her hair / cut*)

2 Sorry about the noise I .... at the moment. (*my roof / repair*)

3 My living room looks fantastic. I .... last week. (*it / paint*)

4 It's Friday so I .... tonight. (*a takeaway / deliver*)

5 I can't talk now because I .... I'll call you back when I've finished. (*eyes / test*)

6 There's something wrong with my car so I .... tomorrow. (*it / repair*).

7 Complete the second sentence so it means the same as the first. Use no more than three words.

1 The Dubai mall has over 750,000 visitors a week. It has around 1,200 shops.

The Dubai mall, ... has around 1,200 shops, has over 750,000 visitors a week.

2 The builders didn't manage to finish the building on time.

The builders weren't .... the building on time.

3 A magazine has named the mall as the 'Best shopping experience'.

The mall .... by a magazine as the 'Best shopping experience'.

4 Someone can style your hair at one of the many beauty salons.

You can have .... at one of the many beauty salons.

5 If you don't enjoy shopping, you probably won't like the Dubai Mall.

If you don't enjoy shopping, you'll probably .... the Dubai Mall.

8 Read the text below and choose the correct word for each space. Mark the correct letter A–D.

Important skills for business

Although every company is different and looks **(1)** .... employees with particular skills related to its business, there are some skills that all employees need to have in their careers. For example, it is important for workers to **(2)** .... good communication skills **(3)** .... they can talk to other employees and their customers effectively. People with these skills will generally **(4)** .... in their jobs more quickly than those people **(5)** .... skills are poor. Employees also need to be **(6)** .... : to plan things carefully and without mistakes. Finally, in most jobs these days, it is necessary to be computer **(7)** .... as companies use more advanced technology.

Managers will need **(8)** .... skills, such as the ability to solve problems and lead a team. A good leader must **(9)** .... motivate a group of people so that their work is **(10)** .... to a high standard. This will benefit the company and help the employees achieve job satisfaction.

	A	B	C	D
1	on	for	about	from
2	be	make	take	have
3	so	because	however	to
4	succeed	achieve	manage	win
5	who	which	whose	that
6	curious	organised	punctual	sensitive
7	careful	intelligent	brilliant	literate
8	as well	further	besides	in addition
9	be able to	was able to	can	could
10	finish	completed	ended	make

A small world

11

Reading
Multiple choice (Part 4)

1 Work in pairs. What places around the world would you like to visit? Why? Would you like to live in a tourist area? Why/Why not?

2 Read the text and questions. For each question mark the correct letter A–D.

1 What is the writer trying to do in this text?

    A Warn people against travelling to the Amazon.

    B Report the decision of a village in the Amazon.

    C Describe the negative effects of tourism in the Amazon.

    D Explain why the Amazon is a dream destination.

2 Nazareth residents believe that visitors

    A aren't interested in seeing how they live.

    B take more photos of animals than people.

    C enjoy photographing the local wildlife.

    D deal with people and animals in the same way.

3 What does the situation in Nazareth say about people in other towns nearby?

    A They agree about the effects of tourism.

    B They have planned for their development.

    C They take different views on tourism.

    D They think the role of tourism is important.

4 What do we learn about the increase in tourism?

    A It has not benefitted everyone.

    B It will have a negative effect on wildlife.

    C It was not predicted by local people.

    D It has been welcomed by everyone.

5 What might a tourist say about a visit to Nazareth?

    A It's a long boat ride from the nearest city but it's worth it.

    B The local people refused to let us ask them questions.

    C The residents were given money by our travel agent.

    D Travellers aren't allowed to swim with the local sea life.

> **EXAM TIP**
>
> Questions 2, 3 and 4 ask about specific information or opinions and follow the order of information in the text.

The jungle town lost to tourists

RESIDENTS HAVE HAD ENOUGH OF **BADLY-BEHAVED** VISITORS

The small Amazonian town of Nazareth, just a **20-minute** boat ride from the Colombian jungle town of Leticia, is a traveller's dream. But tourists might have to give the place a miss in future as residents have chosen to refuse entry to travellers. Their main reasons are the tourists' behaviour, and the fact that they get just a little of the money tourists spend in the area.

Nazareth residents say that most of the tourists' money goes to travel agencies and not locals. They also believe some tourists can't see the difference between the wildlife and residents, taking photos of local families as if they were just another kind of animal. And what a tourist may think are polite, curious questions about the local culture, often make them seem rude to local people.

The actions taken by the Nazareth townspeople have uncovered a difference of opinion among residents in local Amazon towns about what role tourism should play in the region's development. With the rise of eco-tourism, this part of the Amazon has seen more travellers arrive to swim with the **world-famous** pink dolphins, hike through the rainforests and admire the **brightly-lit** water as the sun rises.

An amazing 35,000 people travelled to the region last year; five times more than in the whole of the previous eight years. But as Nazareth residents complain, the local people have so far seen few of the benefits and mostly just the disadvantages.

Residents in other towns, however, believe the number of visitors to the region is going to rise whatever they do, so they should try to make money from it. They believe that **well-controlled** tourism can help improve living conditions in the area.

Speaking

3 **Work in pairs and discuss the questions.**

1 Do you think the residents of Nazareth made a good decision? Why/Why not?

2 How could Amazon townspeople control tourism and increase the money they earn from it?

Vocabulary
Compound adjectives

4 **Complete the sentences with an appropriate compound adjective in bold in the text.**

1 The zoo is a .... bus ride from the hotel.

2 Everyone looked up at the .... sky.

3 City residents often complain about .... tourists.

4 The Eiffel Tower is a .... tourist attraction.

5 There is a .... system for visiting the Galapagos islands.

5 **Complete the compound adjectives in each sentence with a word from the list.**

behaved	efficient	fashioned	made
paid	service	up	way

1 I'd love to buy a one-........................ plane ticket to the other side of the world.

2 I'd be happy to have a badly-........................ job if I lived on a tropical island.

3 I go to self-........................ restaurants on holiday where I can eat all I want.

4 I try to use energy-........................ transport when I travel.

5 I usually buy local hand-........................ holiday souvenirs for my family.

6 I like learning about past traditions of a culture, even if they're old-........................ now.

7 I'm always well-........................ when I travel abroad.

8 I don't like spending time in built-........................ areas.

6 **Work in pairs. Take turns to guess whether each sentence in Activity 5 is true or false for your partner. Do you know your partner better than he/she knows you?**

Travel and transport

1 **Work in pairs and discuss the questions.**

1 What do you enjoy about travelling?

2 What do you dislike about travelling?

2 **Read the article. Which finalist would you vote for? Why?**

Top Travel Apps Award

Vote for your favourite travel app of the year and you could win €500. Here are the lucky finalists.

Footstep – View beautiful photos from the brochures of over 50 sightseeing destinations before you even ¹**set off**. ²**Look for** the best shops and markets to buy a few souvenirs, and ³**get rid of** your heavy old guidebook!

Trip Guide – This helpful app reads your email holiday reservation and sends the information back as one simple travel timetable. It'll even copy in the people ⁴**picking** you **up** from the airport at the end of your trip. It'll also email you the daily exchange rate.

The Ski Club – As well as live snow reports, they've ⁵**set** webcams **up** in many popular skiing destinations so you'll never ⁶**end up** on a snowless mountain again.

Locator – This app lets you ⁷**turn** your photos **into** unforgetable memories. Take a photo of your surroundings, then use this app to add comments so you won't forget where you were when you ⁸**catch up with** friends.

3 **Complete the sentences with a highlighted noun from the text in Activity 2 and a verb from the list.**

buy	get	make	publish	read	take

1 I think hotels are sometimes dishonest in the .... they ....

2 I like to .... to remind me of places I visit.

3 I prefer to .... a .... about a place before I go.

4 I only .... a .... after doing hours of online research.

5 I'd love to .... a .... around the world.

6 You can .... a good .... with the dollar at the moment.

4 **Work in pairs. Are the statements in Activity 3 true for you?**

Phrasal verbs of travel

5 **Match the phrasal verbs in the Activity 2 text (1–8) with the meanings A–H.**

A collect someone or something

B talk to someone after an absence

C place something somewhere

D start a journey

E try to find something

F throw away something you don't want anymore

G be somewhere you didn't plan

H become something different

6 **Complete the table with phrasal verbs 1–8 from Activity 2.**

1 with no object
set off ....
2 verb + preposition/adverb + object
....
3 verb + object + preposition/adverb
....
4 verb + two prepositions/adverbs
....

LANGUAGE TIP

When phrasal verbs are followed by a verb, use the -ing form. *We ended up **walking** home.*

7 **Complete the gaps with a phrasal verb from Activity 5.**

1 Do you enjoy .... on a journey really early in the morning? Why/Why not?

2 Have you ever been on a journey and .... in the wrong place? What happened?

3 When you arrive in a new town, what are the first things you .... ? Why?

4 Who do you usually call when you want someone to .... you .... ? Why?

5 What are the first things you talk about when you .... friends after travelling? Why?

6 Do you ever .... souvenirs after a few months? Why/Why not?

7 Have you ever .... a short trip .... a longer stay? What happened?

8 If you could .... a webcam anywhere in the world, where would it be? Why?

8 **Discuss the questions in Activity 7 in pairs.**

Listening
Multiple choice (Part 1)

1 Work in pairs. Which of the objects in the box do you think is the most important to take on holiday? Why?

a camera   your mobile   a guidebook

2 ▶ 54 Listen to two people discussing the question in Activity 1. Which object do they agree on?

3 ▶ 55 Listen to the recording. For each question there are three pictures and a short recording. Choose the correct picture.

1 What part of the man's body hurts?

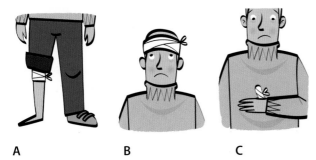

A   B   C

2 Who is in the photograph?

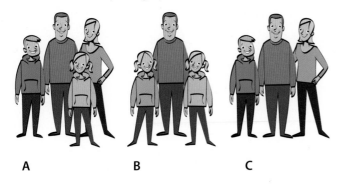

A   B   C

3 Which homework will the man do tonight?

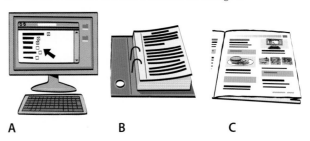

A   B   C

4 Which sport is free to try today?

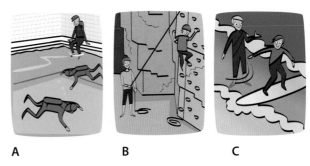

A   B   C

5 When can the public start using the new IT Centre?

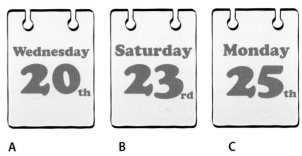

A   B   C

6 What do the women eat for lunch?

A   B   C

7 What does the boy want to send back?

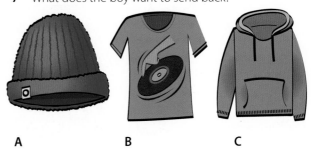

A   B   C

Speaking

1 **Work in pairs and discuss the questions.**

1 What animals do you like? Which animals frighten you?

2 What do you know about the animal in the photo?

2 **Read the advert. What is it advertising?**

3 **Read the article again and decide if the statements are correct (A) or incorrect (B).**

1 Chris thinks the money spent on pandas is wasted.

2 Chris says people pay less for dead tigers.

3 Mark blames people for the problems pandas have.

Future forms

▶ **GRAMMAR** REFERENCE p.131

4 **Match the future forms 1–4 in bold in the article to uses A–D.**

A A future arrangement (everything has been organised)

B A future intention (nothing has been organised)

C A timetabled event (e.g. start/finish days and times)

D A prediction (something you think will happen)

LANGUAGE TIP

When we talk about future intentions with *go* and *come*, we often use the present continuous instead of *going to*. *Are you going to the conference next month?*

5 **Choose the most appropriate future form in each comment.**

1 'I think the wildlife projects .... (*increase*) the number of pandas in future so Chris is talking rubbish.'

2 'I think Chris is absolutely right so I .... (*stop*) giving money to animal charities as soon as possible.'

3 'I .... (*attend*) the conference in Sheffield and have already signed up on the website. It .... (*start*) at 10 a.m. if you're interested.'

4 'I .... (*fly*) to India on Tuesday to start a wildlife project. I'm sure my work .... (*be*) useful.'

Speaking

6 **Work in pairs and discuss the questions.**

1 Do you agree or disagree with Chris Packham's view on pandas? Why/Why not?

2 What other wild animals around the world do you think will die out in future? Why?

3 Which features of our world are going to disappear if they're not protected? Why?

Students' Union Animal Protection Society

SUAPS 🐾

STUDENTS' UNION ANIMAL PROTECTION SOCIETY

Should we save the panda?

Wildlife charities around the world [1]**are going to spend** millions of pounds on conserving the panda over the next ten years. But is this worth the money?

Wildlife expert and animal lover Chris Packham thinks not, and believes we should leave pandas to die out, because the money can be better spent on other wildlife projects. He also believes the tiger [2]**will die out** in the next 15 years whatever we do, as it is impossible to protect an animal that is worth more dead than alive. Conservation adviser Dr Mark Wright disagrees and suggests that protecting these animals is our responsibility because without humans, their lives wouldn't be in danger.

Students across the country [3]**are meeting to discuss** this and other wildlife topics at a two-day conference in Sheffield. It [4]**starts** on Wednesday 23rd February at the City Star Hotel, Sheffield. Why not come along and join the debate? Go to www.suaps.org for more details.

Speaking
Extended turn (Part 3)

1 **Work in pairs. Student A read questions 1–8. Listen to Student B and make notes. Student B describe the photo above for one minute.**

1 Does your partner start by summarising the content of the photo?

2 Does he/she describe different parts of the photo in detail?

3 Does he/she use a lot of different adjectives?

4 Does he/she use some prepositions of place (e.g. *behind, below*)?

5 Does he/she use modals of possibility (e.g. *could, must, can't*) to guess information?

6 Does he/she make a lot of grammar mistakes or vocabulary mistakes?

7 Does he/she pause a lot, or does he/she speak quite fluently?

8 Is his/her pronunciation clear? Does he/she sound interesting?

2 **Work in pairs. Student B read questions 1–8 in Activity 1. Listen to Student A and make notes. Student A turn to page 121 and describe the photo for one minute.**

3 **Work in pairs. Use your notes from Activities 1 and 2 to tell each other what was good about your descriptions and how you could improve them.**

> **EXAM TIP**
>
> Record yourself and listen back so you can hear what you do well and what you need to improve.

General conversation (Part 4)

4 ▶ **56** **Listen to two candidates talking about what animals they like. What's their favourite? What reasons do they give?**

> **EXAM TIP**
>
> Give reasons for your opinions and ask your partner for his/her reasons to show you can keep a conversation going and interact.

5 **Work in pairs. Talk together about the different kinds of animals you're interested in for three to four minutes. Here are some things you could talk about.**

1 The pets you have had or would like.

2 The animals you have seen or would love to see in the wild.

3 Your views on whether animals should live in zoos or not.

4 Your opinions on why some people want wild animals as pets and whether this is acceptable.

Listening

1 **Work in pairs and discuss the questions.**

1 What new things would you like to see in 25 years?

2 What problems would you like to see disappear?

2 ▶ 57 **You will hear an expert, Professor Allen, talking about planning for city life in the year 2050. While you listen, decide if statements 1–4 are true or false.**

1 Professor Allen thinks governments will measure energy use.

2 He believes the tax system will be different.

3 He is confident that people are going to take more flights in the future.

4 He predicts that supermarkets will be bigger.

will and going to

▶ **GRAMMAR** REFERENCE p.132

3 **Look at the sentences from the listening and underline the future forms.**

A By then, it'll be too late to think, 'Okay, I'll change my life!'

B Most of the world's oil's going to run out by 2050.

C I expect that there'll be taxes on the energy we use.

D I'm going to ride home after this interview!

4 **Use the examples from Activity 3 to complete the table with *will* or *going to*.**

verb form	use
1	predictions with good evidence
2	more general predictions
3	decisions we make while speaking
4	decisions we made before speaking

5 **Complete the conversation in the correct future form, *will* or *going to*.**

A I've decided that I **(1)** .... *start* buying things that will last longer. I hope it **(2)** .... *cut* my electricity bill and save energy!

B That's a good idea, but I don't think it **(3)** .... *make* any difference. There are so many people on the planet one person can't do much! We **(4)** .... *need* governments to create real change! Like the new underground station that they **(5)** .... *build* one block from your house.

A They are? Really? That's great! I **(6)** .... *save* so much time! But governments can't do everything. It's obvious that all of us **(7)** .... *have* to find new lifestyles.

B Well, I don't know much about science, but I think scientists **(8)** .... *provide* the solutions not us! Governments just need to work with the scientists.

LANGUAGE TIP

When you speak, you can pronounce *going to* + verb as '*gonna*'. *I'm **gonna** see my friend later.* You can't contract *going to* + place. *I'm **going to** Spain next week.*

6 **Complete the sentences with a positive or negative future form to make predictions that you believe.**

1 Families .... more time together. (*spend*)

2 People working in the same company .... through the internet, not face to face. (*talk*)

3 Emails .... by video calls. (*be replaced*)

4 We .... a female president of the United Nations. (*have*)

5 All companies .... to show that they have a good environmental record. (*need*)

6 Women's sports .... as well as men's sports. (*pay*)

7 **Work in pairs. Compare your predictions with your partner, and give reasons for your choice.**

8 **Add four more predictions to the list. Which do you think are more likely to come true?**

Speaking

1 **Work in pairs and discuss the questions.**

1 What was the last big change in your city/country?

2 How did you feel about the change at the time? How do you feel now?

Writing

Informal letter (Part 3)

▶ **WRITING** REFERENCE p.147

2 **Look at the exam task. What's Tamsin worried about?**

> This is part of a letter you receive from your English friend, Tamsin, asking for your advice.
>
> > Anyway, I'm a bit worried because I'm going to have to make some big changes next year. Have you decided to change anything recently? Let me know what it is. Are you happy about the change?
>
> Now write a letter to your friend, answering your friend's questions.
>
> Write a **letter** in about **100 words**.

3 **Look at the student answer. Complete the answer with the informal linkers in the box.**

Anyway   At first   At least   Well
You know how

Hi Tamsin

Thanks for you letter. I agree with you, change can be horrible!

What's new with me? **(1)** .... , my city are going to close the road where I live once a week on Sundays. **(2)** .... busy Bogota gets, and I love driving to the shops at the weekend! I'm going to have to travel by bike instead.

(3) .... I hated the idea, but there are lots of other streets which are already closed to cars on Sundays, and they're so popular. There's a real carnival atmosphere. So, I've decided that I'm going to join them and get a new bike. **(4)** .... it's going to help make me a bit fitter!

(5) .... , let me know how it goes with your plans.

Love

Maria Alejandra

EXAM TIP

Linkers like *however* and *in addition* are rather too formal for a letter to a friend. Use informal linkers such as *but* and *too* instead.

4 **Which sentence in each pair contains more informal language?**

1 A In my opinion, you should talk to your friend.

   B I guess the best thing is to talk to your friend.

2 A Write back soon.

   B I look forward to hearing from you.

3 A I have a good relationship with my brother.

   B I get on well with my brother.

4 A I've decided to go for the engineering course.

   B I've selected the engineering course.

5 **Write your answer to Tamsin's letter.**

6 **When you have finished, read your letter again.**

1 Underline the informal language and the linkers.

2 If you didn't use any informal language or linkers, can you find a place to add them?

Extreme

12

Reading

1 Work in pairs and describe the man in the photograph. What's unusual about him? How do you think he's able to do this?

2 Look at the title and subheadings of the article. What do you think the three men's super powers are? Read the article and check if your predictions were correct.

3 Work in pairs and discuss the questions.
1 Which of these skills is the most amazing?
2 Which of these skills would you like to have?

Sport Xtreme

9:25 89%

July issue **Past issues** **Subscriptions**

We're all good at something, but these guys are superhuman

Liew Thow Lin – The Human Magnet
Malaysian Liew Thow Lin has a rare super power. [1]*When he gets near metal, it sticks to him.*

Nobody knows for sure why this happens.

Ma Xiangang – The Electric Man
Ma Xiangang thought he was an ordinary man until he had to fix his TV in China.
He discovered that [2]*if he touches live electricity wires, he feels no pain at all.* In fact, [3]*if he holds two wires in his hands, he can light a bulb.*

Wim Hof – The Human Ice Cube
[4]*If someone falls into icy water, they'll probably become too tired to swim after 15 minutes.* [5]*They'll be dead unless they're rescued within 45 minutes.* But Dutchman Wim Hof can stay completely covered in iced water for up to two hours without any kind of discomfort. Mr Hof says he uses the power of his mind to control his body.

»Next   **»More**   **»Summer**   **»Winter**

Listening
True/False (Part 4)

4 ▶ **58** **You are going to listen to two friends, Jane and Ed, talking about another person with superhuman abilities. Listen to the first part of the recording. What did Mr Velu do?**

EXAM TIP

Listen closely to the first moments of the recording. They should clearly tell you the topic the two people are discussing.

5 ▶ **59** **Now listen to the whole recording and decide if each sentence is correct or incorrect. If it is correct, put a tick (✓) in the box under A for YES. If it is incorrect, put a tick (✓) in the box under B for NO.**

		A	B
1	Ed was surprised after learning about Mr Velu's abilties.	☐	☐
2	Jane thinks Mr Velu can make money from his abilities.	☐	☐
3	They agree that anyone can get strong if they want to.	☐	☐
4	Jane thinks that only a few people have secret abilities.	☐	☐
5	Ed thinks we'll see more unusual abilities in future.	☐	☐
6	They both want to read more about Mr Velu.	☐	☐

Zero and first conditionals
▶ **GRAMMAR** REFERENCE p.132

6 **Look at sentences 1–5 in the article in Activity 2 and answer the questions.**

1 Which sentences describe something that is always true?

2 Which sentences describe something which might happen in the future?

7 **Complete the rules with the correct words.**

_____

present simple   future verb form
_____

1 We use *When / If / Unless* + ... + ...
for things which are always true.

2 We use *If / Unless* + ... + ...
for possibilities in the future.

LANGUAGE TIP

The *If* clause can come first or second in the sentence. When it comes first, you need a comma between the clauses, e.g. *I'll go* **if** *you want.* **If** *you want, I'll go.*

8 **Look at the sentences about some other people who have superhuman abilities. Put the verbs in the sentences in the correct tense.**

1 If you .... (*give*) David Tammet a new language to learn, he .... (*be able*) to hold a conversation in it the next day.

2 If Daniel Browning .... (*get*) locked out of his home tonight, he .... (*squeeze*) through the 50 cm wide window he leaves open.

3 Whenever animal expert Kevin Richardson .... (*come*) face-to-face with a lion, he .... (*use*) his physical strength to fight it.

4 When Tim Cridland .... (*cut*) himself, he .... (*not feel*) pain.

5 If Liam Hoekstra .... (*go*) to the gym later today, he .... (*bend*) the metal equipment, instead of using it.

6 If Jez Rose .... (*tell*) his friends to do something, they .... (*probably not do*) it.

9 **Work in pairs. Do you think the sentences about other 'super' people in Activity 8 are true or false? Check your answers on page 122.**

10 **What advice would you give to someone in these situations? Write sentences starting *If you...* .**

1 getting stronger and fitter

2 learning to swim

3 collecting money for charity

4 finding a rich partner

Speaking

1 Work in pairs. How do you think you would react if you were in extreme danger? Would you be brave? Would you know what to do?

2 Complete the Extreme Danger Quiz on page 123.

Listening

3 ▶ 60 Listen to a survival expert discussing the situations in the quiz in Activity 2 on a radio programme and check your answers.

4 Work in pairs. Which of the situations in Activity 2 would be the worst for you? Why?

Reading
Multiple choice (Part 1)

5 Match the phrases 1–5 with a phrase A–E that has the same meaning.

1   Shallow water. No diving.
2   Dangerous corner ahead.
3   Mobile phones must not be used in the hospital.
4   No entry except for card holders.
5   You must visit your doctor.

A   It's necessary to get medical advice.
B   Some electronic equipment is not allowed here.
C   Watch out for what is in front of you.
D   It isn't deep enough to jump in here.
E   Only certain people are permitted to go in.

> **EXAM TIP**
>
> The correct option does not usually have the same words as the ones in the text. Look for the words in the message and option with the same meaning.

6 Look at the texts in the exam paper. Where would you see each one? Can you think of a different way to phrase the main message in each text?

7 Read each text again and choose the correct letter A–C.

1

DANGER
Machinery may start without warning

A   Don't start the machine without telling people first.
B   Take care because the machine could start at any time.
C   When you hear a warning sound, the machine will start.

2

For safety reasons, gym members are required to wear suitable clothing at all times

A   Wearing sports clothes in the gym is often a good idea.
B   Some gym clothes are more suitable than others.
C   You must always wear sensible clothes in the gym.

3

To: Mrs Williams
From: Broadhill Travel Agency
We are very sorry but due to strong winds, the whale-watching boat trip you booked has been cancelled.

The travel agency

A is suggesting that Mrs Williams travel to see whales by boat.

B is telling Mrs Williams that she cannot go on her planned trip.

C is warning Mrs Williams there'll be storms during her voyage.

4

Pedestrians are **NOT** permitted to cross the railway tracks while the alarm is ringing

A You cannot walk across the tracks when you hear the alarm.

B You can only walk across the tracks when the alarm rings.

C It's not necessary to stop walking when the alarm starts ringing.

5

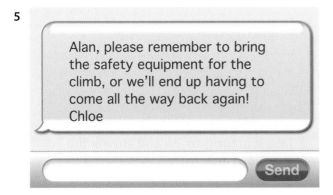

Alan, please remember to bring the safety equipment for the climb, or we'll end up having to come all the way back again!
Chloe

In her message, Chloe

A recommends that Alan use safety equipment.

B remembers when Alan forgot the safety equipment.

C reminds Alan to take the safety equipment.

Vocabulary
Confusing words

8 Work in pairs. Complete the pairs of sentences with the words in the box from Activity 7.

bring   come   go   remembers
reminds   take   travel   trip

1 A I always .... my mobile with me when I .... out.

B I often forget to .... my book when I .... to this lesson.

2 A I regularly .... to other towns and cities.

B I'm going on a business .... next week.

3 A My closest friend never .... to buy me a birthday card.

B My closest friend .... me to call my parents every Sunday.

9 Look at these pairs of confusing words. Put the correct word in each pair in the appropriate sentence. Change the verb form where necessary.

1 *work/job*

A I've got a lot of .... to do today.

B I'd like to get a new ....

2 *come/go*

A I .... to class early today so I could finish my homework.

B I want to .... to the cinema next weekend.

3 *lend/borrow*

A I never .... money to friends.

B I don't like to .... money from friends.

4 *lose/miss*

A I sometimes .... the bus and get to college late.

B I often .... things and find them days later in unusual places.

5 *live/stay*

A On holiday, we usually .... in a small hotel.

B I still .... in my childhood home.

10 Work in pairs. Which statements in Activity 9 are true for you? Change the other statements so they are true for you. Do you and your partner agree?

Listening

1 **Work in pairs and discuss the questions.**

1 Where do you think the places in the pictures are?

2 What do you think life is like for people who live there?

2 ▶ 61 **Listen to Anna and Luke talking about two extreme places. Where would they prefer to live?**

3 **Listen again and answer the questions about each of the two places.**

1 Where is it located?

2 How many people live there?

3 What work do the locals do?

Second conditional

▶ **GRAMMAR** REFERENCE p.132

4 **Look at sentences A–C from the listening and answer questions 1–4.**

A If I had to choose, I'd go for the island.

B I wouldn't live there if you paid me a million pounds!

C If I had enough money, I'd visit both of them.

1 Are the situations described real or unreal/unlikely?

2 Are they in the past or present/future?

3 What verb form is used in the *if* clause?

4 In the main clause of sentences A and C, what does *'d* mean? Is it followed by the infinitive or *-ing* form?

5 **Work in pairs. Student A, look at questions 1–6. Student B, look at the questions on page 123. Use the verbs in brackets to complete the second conditional questions.**

1 If you .... visit Tristan da Cunha or the Hanging Temple, which .... you .... ? (*have to/choose*)

2 Where .... you .... if you .... a million pounds? (*travel/won*)

3 If you .... stuck on a desert island, who .... you .... with you? (*be/want*)

4 How .... you .... if you .... far from your family? (*manage/live*)

5 If you .... an extreme sport on holiday, which one .... you .... ? (*can try/do*)

6 What .... you .... if your car .... in the desert? (*do/break down*)

6 **Take it in turns to ask and answer the questions in Activity 5.**

Speaking

1 **Work in pairs and answer the questions.**

1 What do you know about the landscape in different parts of New Zealand?

2 What activities do you think you could do there?

3 Do you think New Zealand would be a good place to visit? Why/Why not?

Listening

2 ▶ **62** **Listen to two candidates talking about Fiordland in New Zealand. Do both candidates want to go there? Why/Why not?**

3 **Listen again and answer the questions about the female candidate.**

1 Does she use simple sentences or longer sentences with linking words?

2 Does she ask her partner questions?

3 Does she sound interested in the conversation?

Speaking

Simulated situation (Part 2)

▶ **FUNCTIONS** BANK p.154

4 **Work in pairs. Look at the exam task, and talk together for around three minutes.**

You are going to study in New Zealand together for a month. After your course, you want to take a trip together. Talk together about the different places you could visit and decide which one would be best.

EXAM TIP

The examiner will assess your grammar, vocabulary, organisation of ideas, pronunciation and how well you communicate with your partner. Try to get a good balance between these things.

Listening

1 **Work in pairs and answer the questions.**

1 What's the most dangerous sport you've tried? Did you enjoy it? Why/Why not?

2 Look at the photo. What sport does it show? What are the dangers of this sport?

2 ▶ **63** **Listen to four people talking about the sports they do. When did each person start doing them?**

3 **Work in groups. Which of the four sports would most people in the group like to try? Why?**

Sport and leisure

4 **Complete each summary of the listening texts with words related to sport and leisure from the list.**

compete	entered	experienced	fitness
instructor	joined in	practice	practise
prize	safety	taken part in	trained

A Ruby became a ski **(1)** .... after years of **(2)** .... She does extreme skiing because it's challenging. She says that only very **(3)** .... skiers should try it.

B Zac used to **(1)** .... against other people in road races and **(2)** .... hard but he wasn't good enough to win so he started mountain biking. He said that anyone who's **(3)** .... downhill mountain biking knows how dangerous it can be.

C Clare started walking to improve her **(1)** .... She suggests that extreme walkers have to **(2)** .... using **(3)** .... equipment before they start walking.

D Lee **(1)** .... with his friends who were big wave surfing. He's improved a lot and won a **(2)** .... for the best newcomer in a competition he **(3)** .... last year.

5 **Listen again and check your answers.**

do, go, play

6 **Look at the sports and leisure activities in the box. Does each one go with the verb *do*, *go* or *play*?**

athletics	baseball	basketball	dancing	fishing
golf	gymnastics	hockey	horse-riding	jogging
karate	rugby	sailing	squash	table tennis	yoga

> **LANGUAGE TIP**
>
> We usually use *play* with games and ball sports; *go* with activities that end in *-ing*; and *do* with other leisure activities or non-ball/team sports.

7 **Work in pairs and answer the questions.**

1 Which of the sports in Activity 6 have you taken part in? Did you enjoy them?

2 Which sports would you like to try? Why?

3 Have you ever entered a sports competition? Did you win any prizes?

8 ▶ **64** **Listen to Speakers 1–6. Which sports and leisure activities from Activity 6 are they describing? Which words tell you this?**

9 **Work in pairs and follow the instructions.**

1 Choose a sport or leisure activity from Activity 6 but do not tell your partner which one.

2 Take it in turns to ask each other *yes/no* questions about this sport until you guess it correctly.

3 The first person in each pair to guess correctly wins.

EXAM TIP

Pay attention to the meaning of the first sentence. Make sure that you don't change it.

3 Here are some sentences about the cycle race the Tour de France. For each question, complete the second sentence so that it means the same as the first. Use no more than three words.

0 *No other sport race is as demanding as the Tour de France. The Tour de France is* __the most__ *demanding race in the world.*

1 What distance do professional cyclists ride in the Tour? How .... do professional cyclists ride in the Tour?

2 In order to win the Tour, athletes need to have a team to help them.
Athletes cannot win the Tour .... a team to help them.

3 During a race, cyclists can use up to 5,000 calories.
Cyclists use up to 5,000 calories .... are racing.

4 Seven hours of sleep is too little for most racers.
Seven hours of sleep isn't .... for most racers.

5 When scientists tested cyclist Miguel Indurain's heartbeat, they found it was only 28 beats per minute.
When cyclist Miguel Indurain's heartbeat .... , it was only 28 beats per minute.

4 Work in pairs and discuss the questions.

1 Do you agree that the Tour de France is the most difficult sports competition in the world?

2 How important is winning?

5 Imagine you've received a email from your Australian friend, Sam. Write a reply, answering his questions, in about 100 words.

So, that's my favourite sport. In your next letter, perhaps you could tell me a bit about a sport that you find exciting? Why do you like it so much?

Speak to you soon!

Sam

Speaking

1 Work in pairs. Look at the sports.

rowing   cycling   running

1 Which do you think uses the most energy? Why?

2 Which do you think is the most dangerous? Why?

Writing

Sentence transformations (Part 1)

2 Look at the sentences about cycling. Work in pairs and discuss the choices. Which one completes the second sentence so it means the same as the first? Why?

1 It was the first cycle race I had entered.
I .... a cycle race before. (*had entered / was in / hadn't entered*)

2 I don't enjoy other sports as much as cycling.
I think other sports are .... enjoyable than cycling. (*more / as / less*)

1 **Match the beginnings 1–8 with the endings A–H to make complete sentences.**

1   New York State is the third most built-

2   At its northern point, it's just a two-

3   The people who live there are fairly well-

4   The City of New York is world-

5   Up to 3,000 immigrants arrived on a one-

6   The system of immigration was not very well-

7   Many people think of the brightly-

8   But there are towns in the mountains which are old-

A   way ticket every day in the last century.

B   famous for being the heart of the USA.

C   lit streets of the city when they think of New York.

D   controlled in those days.

E   up state in the USA.

F   fashioned and haven't changed much in years.

G   behaved compared to other states, crime is low.

H   minute drive across the border to Canada.

2 **Choose the correct future form of the verbs.**

Bill Gates might be the world's best known business man, but there are others we might not have heard of who have a lot in common with him. Take Amrit Sharma, for example. Both he and Bill Gates are very rich, head global IT companies, and both **(1)** .... *(give)* away most of their fortune before they die. At least that's their intention.

Mr Sharma predicts that his country, India, **(2)** .... *(continue)* to grow economically in the next 30 years. It may be the world's third largest economy in our lifetime. It's not surprising that many British IT companies **(3)** .... *(attend)* a global IT conference on the future of technology in India, which **(4)** .... *(start)* next week. Mr Sharma **(5)** .... *(speak)* at the conference on the first day, and will meet national leaders soon after the conference **(6)** .... *(end)*.

After that, according to his diary, Mr Sharma **(7)** .... *(meet)* with social groups to discuss improvements to education in his country, but he won't be worried about languages. Many Indians already speak English fluently, so there **(8)** .... *(be)* few problems discussing business internationally. It's not surprising many think the Indian economy **(9)** .... *(be)* the one to watch in future years. One thing's certain, Mr Sharma **(10)** .... *(enjoy)* the changes.

3 **Look at the blog and complete it with a word from the box. You will need to put the verbs in the correct form.**

brochure   reservation   end up
exchange rate   fifty-minute   get back
guidebooks   pick up   send back   set off

● ● ●   ▶ | Comments

Wednesday 2nd July

Everything started so well. I arrived at the airport with absolutely no local currency. I was able to get a really good **(1)** .... on the dollar from a man at the airport and **(2)** .... to find my hotel. In the hotel's **(3)** .... it said that the hotel was in the heart of the city, but the man at the information desk said it was actually a good **(4)** .... taxi journey from the centre. Anyway, I'd arranged to be collected when I'd made my hotel **(5)** ...., and a rough-looking driver came to **(6)** .... me .... and take me to the hotel. When I went to pay him, he said that the money I had wasn't real, which explains why it was such a good rate! The driver was so angry! We **(7)** .... at a police station while I tried to explain that I wasn't really a criminal. I was nearly in tears, but eventually they let me go and **(8)** .... me .... to my hotel with enough money to pay for the taxi. Of course, when I **(9)** ...., it was too late to eat dinner in the hotel. Next time, I'll only get money out of the places they recommend in the **(10)** ....

4 **Write the verbs in CAPITALS in the correct future form, *will* or *going to*.**

A   So where **(1)** .... you .... on holiday this year?   GO

B   I still haven't decided, but I think I **(2)** .... in Spain again.   END UP

A   **(3)** .... your sister .... there?   BE

B   No, she **(4)** .... friends in Canada in June, and she can't afford both holidays. Come with me!   VISIT

A   Oh, thank you, I'd love to, but I **(5)** .... with my cousins in Australia most of the summer.   STAY

B   Wow. What **(6)** .... you .... there?   DO

A   Well, I think I **(7)** .... the jungle while I'm there. I'd like to, but I haven't really decided.   VISIT

B   You **(8)** .... such an amazing time!   HAVE

5 Put the verbs in the correct tense.

Roadside Attractions

America's famous for road trips. Some of the attractions along the way are worth stopping for.

1 Alongside the Southern Pacific Railroad, you can visit the Beer Can House, which is completely made of beer cans. If a visitor .... (*want*) to go inside, he .... (*have to*) pay a $1 entry fee.

2 The Louisville Slugger Factory is famous for making some of the finest baseball bats in the world. If you .... (*like*) baseball, you .... (*love*) the 40m bat that sits outside their baseball museum.

3 When visitors........................... (*drive*) across the North and South Carolina borders, they .... (*pass*) Pedro the giant Mexican chef, who stands over 30m tall.

4 At night, a huge monster lights up the Delaware skyline. If you .... (*be*) lucky enough to win the NASCAR races in Delaware, you .... (*receive*) a mini statue of the Monster who decorates their roof.

5 It .... (*not be*) possible to move the world's largest ball of string, unless the local mayor of Darwin .... (*bring*) in special lifting equipment. The giant ball took 23 weeks to make!

6 Look at the people discussing the best advice in dangerous situations. Match the first part of the sentence (1–6) with the second part (A–F), and then write the verbs in the correct tense to form the second conditional.

How to survive disaster

1 If you .... (*find*) yourself sinking in mud or sand,

2 If you .... (*be*) caught in falling snow,

3 You .... (*be*) more likely to survive a Tornado

4 You .... (*need*) to get to a tall building if

5 If you .... (*fall*) 50m down,

6 You .... (*escape*) a forest fire without injury

A you ....(*see*) the warning signs of a Tsunami.

B you .... (*probably end up*) buried in snow. Make a hole above your chest and mouth before the snow hardens so you can breathe and shout for help.

C you .... (*need*) to try and land on your feet to survive the landing.

D if you .... (*get*) into a car and .... (*hide*) under a blanket.

E you .... (*need*) to take off anything heavy then 'swim' to the side. The mud isn't usually very deep.

F if you .... (*have*) an underground place to hide.

7 Complete gaps 1–10 with the words A–C.

Tomorrow's holidays

What will the holidays of the future look like? It's a question many people in the travel industry would like to answer. Experts **(1)** .... in Rio de Janeiro later this month to predict the future of tourism. Many people will be prepared to go further to find that special holiday that they'll never **(2)** .... Some travel experts think that they won't even have to leave the airport **(3)** .... they really want to. Many airports already have excellent entertainment facilities where passengers can play video games and even **(4)** .... jogging while they wait. These are likely to stay popular, with airports giving passengers the opportunity to **(5)** .... in all sorts of sports, from skiing to surfing, in the same destination. Guests will be able to **(6)** .... equipment, and even clothes, to reduce the amount of luggage that they take on planes. The **(7)** .... itself will be better for the environment, with biofuels powering airplanes. As companies **(8)** .... to build the most energy-efficient hotels, not a drop of water or electricity **(9)** .... wasted. Cruise ships have been the big success story for holidays over the last few years. In future, floating islands where people can go to relax and improve their levels of **(10)** .... will be the new cruise.

	A		B		C	
1	meet		are meeting		met	
2	remember		miss		forget	
3	when		if		unless	
4	do		go		play	
5	participate		enter		go	
6	borrow		take		lend	
7	travel		tour		backpacking	
8	join		compete		participate	
9	be		will be		is going to be	
10	fitness		condition		sport	

Communication activities

Unit 1, Vocabulary focus, Activity 2

The big five quiz

Read the sentences under each heading and tick (✓) the ones you agree with.

Open
I have a big vocabulary in my language. ✓
I have a lot of ideas. ☐
I spend time thinking about things. ✓
I use difficult words in my language. ☐
I have a good imagination. ✓

Conscientious
I am always prepared. ✓
I pay attention to details. ✓
I follow a timetable. ✓
I am tidy. ✓
I am responsible. ✓

Extroverted
I talk a lot. ☐
I like meeting new people. ☐
I start conversations. ☐
I talk to a lot of different people at parties. ☐
I am happy when people pay attention to me. ✓

Anxious
I worry about things. ✓
I want to get things right. ✓
I get nervous easily. ☐
I feel other people's feelings. ☐
It is difficult for me to relax. ☐

Agreeable
I am interested in people. ✓
I care about other people's feelings. ☐
I give my time to other people. ✓
I make people feel comfortable. ☐
I don't like feeling alone. ✓

Count how many ticks you have in each section. Three ticks or more in a section means that this is a strong character type for you. Go back to page 9 and read about your strongest character types.

Unit 1, Writing focus, Activity 5

Look at the sample answer below. Where should the paragraph breaks be?

Dear Becky,

Thanks for your letter. It sounds like you and your family have a lot of fun. In my family, I'm closest to my brother, but we haven't got much in common. He's so much more confident than I am, and popular, too. He can be annoying, though. He's really good-looking, but he spends ages worrying about his clothes and hair. There are always loads of girls round our house visiting him, which I always thought was funny! Anyway, I wanted to know what you're planning for your birthday. Tell me next time.

Lots of love,

Lisa

Unit 7, Listening and Grammar focus, Activity 8

Complete the sentences below with *much, many, a few* or *a little*.

1 There were a .... different activities to choose from.
2 There weren't .... people in the pool.
3 I had a .... time to relax before coming home.
4 I made a .... new friends while I was there!
5 There were so .... things happening, I was never bored.
6 There was so .... to do, I had a brilliant time!

Unit 2, Vocabulary and Speaking focus, Activity 10

Student A

Describe this photo to Student B. They will answer questions about your description. Then listen to Student B and answer questions 1–4.

1 Does your partner describe the place and the objects in it?
2 Does your partner say who the people are?
3 Does your partner describe the people?
4 Does your partner say what the people are doing?

Unit 2, Reading focus, Activity 5

How do you think food photographers use the things in these pictures? Student A, turn to page 116. Student B, turn to page 119. Read the blog and tell your partner if your predictions were correct.

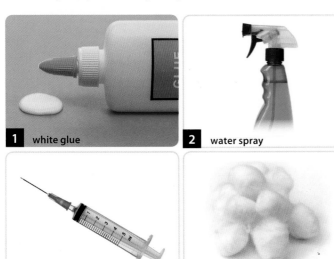

1 white glue
2 water spray
3 syringe
4 cotton wool ball

Unit 8, Grammar focus 1, Activity 7

Student A

1 Look at the people who said the quotes on being famous below. What do you know about them?
2 Tell your partner about the quotes, using reported speech, and discuss what the people said.

> They don't want heroes; what they want is to see you fall.
> **Leonardo DiCaprio, actor**

> I like being famous. It can be a pain but I get free food in restaurants.
> **Noel Gallagher, then guitarist with the band Oasis**

> Hollywood is a place where they'll pay you a thousand dollars for a kiss and fifty cents for your soul.
> **Marilyn Monroe, actor**

Unit 8, Grammar focus 2, Activity 9

Student A

Ask your partner questions 1–5, and answer Student B's questions. Try to remember the answers.

1 Who's your favourite actor or actress? Why?
2 What's your favourite film? Why?
3 Do you like horror films?
4 How often do you see films?
5 What film would you like to see in the near future?

Unit 2, Vocabulary and Speaking focus, Activity 10

Student B

Listen to Student A and answer questions 1–4. Then describe this photo to Student A. They will answer questions about your description.

1 Does your partner describe the place and the objects in it?
2 Does your partner say who the people are?
3 Does your partner describe the people?
4 Does your partner say what the people are doing?

Unit 2, Reading focus, Activity 5

Student A

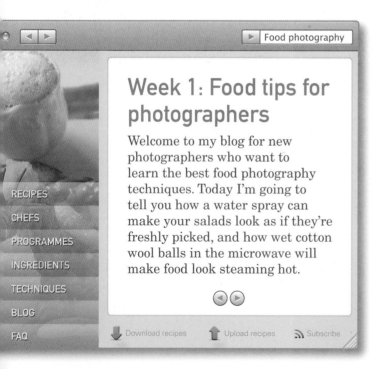

Unit 8, Grammar focus 1, Activity 7

Student B

1 Look at the people who said the quotes on being famous below. What do you know about them?
2 Tell your partner about the quotes, using reported speech, and discuss what the people said.

> You can't be a star at home.
> **Jim Carrey, actor**

> Being famous is just a job.
> **Britney Spears, singer and actor**

> The good part about being famous is being able to help people. The hard part is every day you have to be in a good mood.
> **Michael Jordan, basketball player**

Unit 8, Grammar focus 2, Activity 9

Student B

Ask your partner questions 1–5, and answer Student A's questions. Try to remember the answers.

1 Who's your favourite band or singer? Why?
2 What's your favourite song? Why?
3 Do you buy CDs or download music?
4 How much do you spend on music each month?
5 What song would you like to buy?

Unit 2, Grammar focus, Activity 4

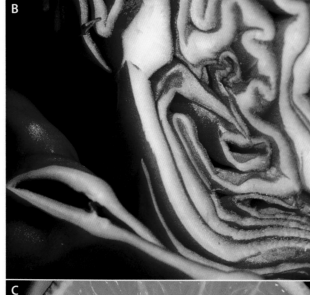

Unit 8, Vocabulary and Speaking focus, Activity 6

Student A

Unit 9, Speaking and Grammar focus, Activity 6

Unit 2, Grammar focus, Activity 6

Work in pairs and discuss. What do you think these photos are of? Use modals such as *could be, must be* and *can't be* to sound more natural. Turn to page 122 and check.

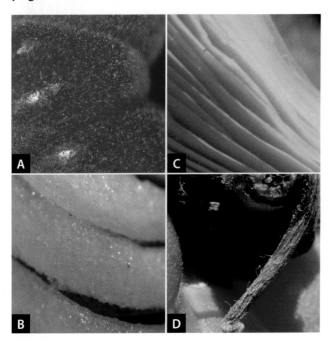

Unit 4, Grammar focus 2, Activity 6

Unit 3, Grammar focus, Activity 7

Online Friends APPLICATION FORM

Thank you for your interest in Online Friends. To help us match you to the perfect friend, please complete the sentences below.

1 I dislike ....
2 I practise .... a lot.
3 I'd really like .... next year.
4 I think it's important for a friend ....
5 I'm interested in ....
6 I'm afraid of ....
7 My typical day involves ....
8 .... is an activity that I love doing.

Unit 4, Grammar focus 1, Activity 7

Complete the article with the present perfect or past simple form of the verb in brackets. Would you like to visit this exhibition?

Bring-a-thing-a-thon

An unusual exhibition (1)............................. (*just/open*) in London where members of the public are providing the objects for the show. Before opening, organisers of the project (2)............................. (*invite*) visitors to 'bring a thing' that was no bigger than their head.

The *Things* exhibition forms part of the Wellcome Collection of over one and a half million objects that once (3)............................. (*belong*) to Sir Henry Wellcome, a successful pharmacist who famously (4)............................. (*collect*) things related to science and medicine.

Visitors to the exhibition (5)............................. (*already/bring*) in strange, interesting and everyday things. For example, an old toy that the owner (6)............................. (*have*) since he was five years old, a hat that (7)............................. (*travel*) around the world and a camera that the owner (8)............................. (*buy*) in 1963.

The exhibition is open for another week so there's still time to join in the Bring-a-thing-a-thon.

Unit 9, Speaking and Grammar focus, Activity 7

Look at the photographs of people doing creative activities. Student A: talk about what you can see in photo A.
Student B: listen, then talk about what you can see in photo B.

Unit 2, Reading focus, Activity 5

Student B

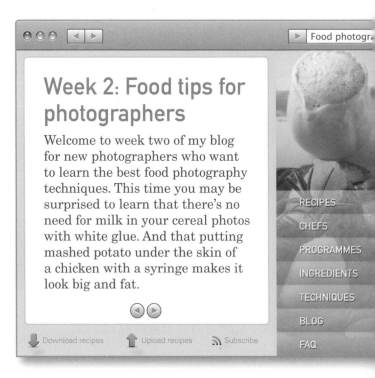

Unit 9, Speaking and Grammar focus, Activity 12

Student A

Guess how many people in the class have/had these abilities. Add two ideas of your own.

1 Swim by the age of six.
2 Play a musical instrument.
3 Do their last homework without checking a dictionary.
4 Build a fire in a forest.
5 ....
6 ....

Unit 5, Vocabulary and Speaking focus, Activity 10

Student A, choose a person in the photo. Student B, ask *yes/no* questions to guess who it is. For example: *Is he wearing a long grey shirt? Does he have black leather shoes?*

Now swap roles. Student B, choose a person in the photo. Student A, ask questions to guess who it is.

Unit 6, Grammar focus, Activity 7

Student A, put the verbs in brackets into the correct past simple or past continuous form. Check your answers with another Student A.

A farmer **(1)** .... (*enjoy*) a nice cup of coffee in front of an open fire when he **(2)** .... (*hear*) a small knock at the door. He **(3)** .... (*open*) the door and looked down to find a snail. The snail **(4)** .... (*shake*) from the cold. 'Could I come into the warm, Sir?' he **(5)** .... (*ask*) the farmer politely. The farmer looked annoyed. 'No, you can't. Get out of here!' he replied and then **(6)** .... (*kick*) the snail across the garden where the grass was cold and wet from the rain. The farmer **(7)** .... (*close*) the door and went back to his fire. Spring **(8)** .... (*arrive*), followed by the summer and then autumn. One day in winter, as snow **(9)** .... (*fall*) heavily and the farmer **(10)** .... (*make*) himself some soup, there was a knock at the door. He **(11)** .... (*open*) it and looked around. No one was there. Eventually, he looked down and **(12)** .... (*see*) a snail. The snail looked up at the farmer, opened his mouth and said angrily, 'Why did you do that?'

Unit 6, Speaking focus, Activity 5

Student A

Phase 1

Ask Student B questions about

1   how long they have been learning English.
2   what qualities you need to be a good learner.
3   what equipment helps them in their studies.

Phase 2

Listen to Student C's answers and note down the discourse markers you hear.

Phase 3

Answer Student C's questions. Try to use discourse markers in your answers.

Unit 9, Speaking and Grammar focus, Activity 12

Student B

Guess how many people in the class have/had these abilities. Add two ideas of your own.

1   Write by the age of five.
2   Wake up easily this morning.
3   Make things with their hands.
4   Easily find their way around a new town.
5   ....
6   ....

Unit 9, Vocabulary focus, Activity 6

Student B

Add the correct prefixes to the words in *italics*.

1   Do people think you're a ....-*confident* person?
2   In your country, is it easy to ....*train* in a new career when you're over 40?
3   What's your dream job? Is it an ....*possible* job for you to do? Why?
4   Have you ever strongly .... *agreed* with your colleagues or classmates?
5   Do you always work, even if you're feeling ....*well*?
6   What's the main .... *advantage* of your choice of work?
7   Is being creative in your job important or ....*important* to you?

Ask your partner the questions. Are you surprised by any of his/her answers?

Unit 6, Vocabulary focus, Activity 7

Student A

Imagine this is Student B's school report, and you are their teacher. Give them feedback on their progress and suggest ways to improve.

SCHOOL REPORT

Attendance: 10%

Attitude to studies: Very poor

Grades in last test: 8/10

Unit 6, Speaking focus, Activity 5

Student B

Phase 1

Answer Student A's questions. Try to use discourse markers in your answers.

Phase 2

Ask Student C questions about

1   a skill they have learnt in their free time.

2   what qualities they need to do that skill.

3   what equipment they need to help them with that skill.

Phase 3

Listen to Student A's answers and note down the discourse markers you hear.

Unit 10, Listening and Grammar focus, Activity 12

Facts about eBay

1   **True**

2   **False** A mobile phone is sold every 6 seconds.

3   **Probably True** This is the average number of bikes sold each hour.

4   **False** eBay sellers are not employed by eBay (if they were, this would be true!).

5   **True** The car owner had an argument with his wife and she sold his car for 50p.

6   **False** It was the most expensive car, but a 405ft mega yacht was sold for over $168 million.

Unit 10, Speaking focus, Activity 8

A student in your class is leaving next week to start university in another town. Talk together about the leaving gifts you could buy for him and then say which one would be best.

Unit 11, Speaking focus, Activity 2

Unit 6, Vocabulary focus, Activity 7

Student B

Imagine this is Student A's school report, and you are their teacher. Give them feedback on their progress and suggest ways to improve.

SCHOOL REPORT

Attendance: 100%

Attitude to studies: Excellent

Grades in last test: 2/10

Unit 12, Listening and Grammar focus, Activity 9

1 **False** David was asked to learn Icelandic, and was able to hold a normal conversation on Icelandic TV an incredible one week later.

2 **True** But Daniel's known as Mr Rubber, and can squeeze through a tennis racquet, which is much smaller.

3 **False** Kevin is known as the Lion Whisperer, and can 'speak' to lions and other large cats, even spending the night sleeping safely with wild lions.

4 **True** Tim is unable to feel pain, no matter how bad the injury.

5 **False** Liam was just six when he could bend metal. He has an unusual muscle disorder and was strong enough to stand up on his own one day after he was born!

6 **False** Jez is a psychologist who is able to use his knowledge of the way the mind works to make people follow any instructions while believing that they chose freely to do it.

Unit 2, Grammar focus, Activity 6

Unit 6, Speaking focus, Activity 5

Student C

Phase 1

Listen to Student B's answers and note down the discourse markers you hear.

Phase 2

Answer Student B's questions. Try to use discourse markers in your answers.

Phase 3

Ask Student A questions about

1 a skill they would like to use at work.

2 what qualities they need to do that skill.

3 what equipment they need to help them with that skill.

Unit 12, Reading focus, Activity 2

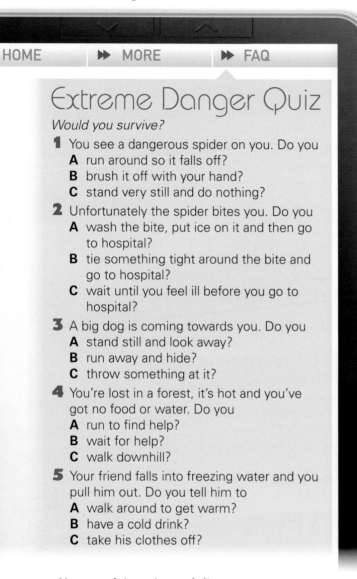

HOME ▶▶ MORE ▶▶ FAQ

Extreme Danger Quiz

Would you survive?

1 You see a dangerous spider on you. Do you
A run around so it falls off?
B brush it off with your hand?
C stand very still and do nothing?

2 Unfortunately the spider bites you. Do you
A wash the bite, put ice on it and then go to hospital?
B tie something tight around the bite and go to hospital?
C wait until you feel ill before you go to hospital?

3 A big dog is coming towards you. Do you
A stand still and look away?
B run away and hide?
C throw something at it?

4 You're lost in a forest, it's hot and you've got no food or water. Do you
A run to find help?
B wait for help?
C walk downhill?

5 Your friend falls into freezing water and you pull him out. Do you tell him to
A walk around to get warm?
B have a cold drink?
C take his clothes off?

Now work in pairs and discuss your answers. Do you agree?

Unit 7, Listening and Grammar focus, Activity 10

11 **You are going on a cruise. Talk together about the different things you could take with you, and decide which five things would be most important. Here are some ideas to help you.**

business card   evening dress or suit
guide book   gym clothes   insect repellent
map   sandals   spare batteries
sun cream   washing powder

Unit 12, Grammar focus, Activity 5

Student B

Use the verbs in brackets to complete the second conditional questions.

1 If you .... live in an extreme place in your country, where .... it .... ? (*have to/be*)

2 If you .... the richest person in the world, where .... you .... to? (*become/move*)

3 If you .... to the moon, ... you .... ? (*can travel/go*)

4 How .... you .... if you .... in a very cold place? (*manage/live*)

5 If you .... any mountain, which one .... you .... ? (*can climb/choose*)

6 What .... you .... if you .... lost on a small boat in the ocean? (*do/be*)

Unit 7, Grammar focus, Activity 5

Complete the second half of the article with the correct answer *a/an*, *the* or (–) for no article.

Mokens dive up to 75 feet under water without oxygen. They collect **(1)** .... fish and **(2)** .... seafood with simple tools. **(3)** .... Swedish scientist decided to investigate the skills Moken children have. She discovered that **(4)** .... children train their eyes to see better underwater than any other humans can.

The Mokens have just a few possessions. They think of themselves as **(5)** .... big family so share what they have with each other. Unfortunately, **(6)** .... life has become more difficult for them. **(7)** .... new laws have been created to protect the environment and so the Mokens can no longer cut down trees to make new boats. This means that they cannot travel around **(8)** .... sea as freely as before to swap fish for food or gasoline. Many Moken people now live in homes on islands around **(9)** .... Thailand. **(10)** .... number of Mokens living the traditional life is just 1000, although leaders are trying to make sure their traditions do not die.

Grammar reference

Unit 1

1.1 Questions

There are three main types of questions:

1 *Yes/No* questions (the expected answer is *yes* or *no*)
   A *Do you like football?*
   B *Yes, I do.*
2 *Wh-* questions (questions with *Who? Whose? Where? Why? What? Which?* and *How?*)
   ***What** do you want?*
   ***Where** are you from?*
   ***When** did you get here today?*
3 Alternative questions (the expected answer is one of two options)
   *Do you want **coffee** or **tea**?*
   *Which do you prefer, **rock** or **Latin** music?*

1.2 Yes/No questions

- To form a question with *be*, *have (got)* and modal verbs like *may, can, could, would*, change the order of the subject and the verb.
  *He's got a new laptop. – **Has he got** a new laptop?*
  ***Are you going** to the party later?*
  ***Should I phone** to apologise?*
  ***Can you swim**?*
- With other verbs, use *Do/Does/Did* + subject + infinitive
  ***Do you know** my brother?*
  ***Does she speak** English?*
  ***Did she tell** you about the homework?*

1.3 Wh- questions

question word/phrase	auxiliary verb	subject	main verb (and the rest)
What	did	you	do (last weekend)?
Where	did	you	go (last Saturday)?
How long	are	you	going (to be here)?
Where	do	you	think (he is)?

With questions about the subject, we don't use an auxiliary and we don't change the order of the subject and verb. The word order is the same as it is for statements.

Questions about the subject
   ***Who saw** James last night?*
   ***What makes** you happy?*
Questions about the object
   ***Who did** James **see** last night?*
   ***What did** you **watch** on TV last night?*

1.4 Alternative questions

There are two types of alternative questions. In one type the word order is like a *Yes/No* question and in the other type the word order is like a *Wh-* question.

   ***Would** you **like** to go to the cinema or to a restaurant?*
   ***What shall** we **do** later, study a bit more or take a break?*

1.5 Indirect questions

USE   We use indirect questions when we're being polite.
Direct question (neutral): *What time is it?*
Indirect question (more polite): *Do you know what time it is?*

FORM

- Don't use the auxiliary verb.
- Don't change the order of the subject and verb. The word order is the same as the statement form.
- When there is no question word and the answer to the question is *yes* or *no*, we use *if* or *whether*.
- Indirect questions often start with *I'd like to know, Do you know, Can you tell me, Could you tell me...? Could* is slightly more polite than *can*.
  ***I'd like to know where** you bought that watch.* (Where did you buy that watch?)
  ***Do you know if** it's going to rain later?* (Is it going to rain later?)
  ***Can you tell me where** the train station is?* (Where's the train station?)
  ***Could you tell me whether** this car is for sale?* (Is this car for sale?)

Unit 2

2.1 Present simple

USE   We use the present simple to talk about
1 Regular repeated actions, routines and habits in the present
   *We **go** to the cinema every Friday.*
   *He **plays** rugby on Saturdays.*
   *They **don't eat** meat.*
2 A permanent situation
   *She **lives** in Prague.*
   *We **come** from a small town in China.*
   *I **don't drive** a car.*
3 In spoken instructions, systems and processes
   *You **put** your money in and then you **press** the button.*
   *You **turn** left and then you **go** straight on.*
4 With state verbs
   *We **know** the train's late.*
   *I don't **own** a TV.*
   *He **agrees** with me.*
   Other state verbs include: *hate, prefer, want, need, mind, understand, taste, smell, hear, disagree, promise, seem.*

FORM With regular verbs, we form the present simple with the base form of the verb. *He/She/It* forms are different.

- Positive statements:
  I/You/We/They **like** *pop music.*
  He/She/It **likes** *pop music.*
- Negative statements:
  I/You/We/They **don't like** *pop music.*
  He/She/It **doesn't like** *pop music.*
- Questions: We use the auxiliary verb *do* to make present simple questions.
  Do *I/you/we/they* **like** *pop music? Yes, I/you/we/they do. No, I/you/we/they* **don't**.
  Does *he/she/it* **like** *pop music? Yes, he/she/it does. No, he/she/it* **doesn't**.

2.2 Present continuous

USE We use the present simple to talk about these things in the present:

1 Actions happening now
   Ken's **reading** *in the living room.*
2 Temporary situations
   Sam's **working** *as a waiter for the summer.*

FORM *be* + *-ing* form.

- Positive statements
  I'm/You're/He's/She's/It's/We're/They're + *-ing* form
  He's **studying** *English.*
- Negative statements
  I'm not/You aren't/He isn't/She isn't/It isn't/We aren't/They aren't + *-ing* form
  I'm **not driving** *to work at the moment as my car's broken down.*
- Questions
  The subject and the verb *be* are inverted.
  Are you *staying at a hotel?*
  Is he *riding his motorbike?*

2.3 Adverbs of frequency

USE We use adverbs of frequency to talk about how often an action happens.
   always, usually, often, sometimes, occasionally, rarely, never, every Monday evening, twice a year

FORM

1 Adverbs of frequency usually come
- after an auxiliary verb
  We **don't usually** *cook on a Sunday.*
- after the verb *to be*
  He's **rarely** *at home at the weekends.*
- before all other verbs
  I **occasionally download** *music.*
  She **sometimes does** *her homework.*

2 Usually, often, sometimes and occasionally can also come at the beginning or end of a clause in spoken English.
   Sometimes, *we get home early.*
   My friends call me **occasionally**.
3 Always and never come in the middle of a clause.
   I **always** *drink my coffee black.*
4 Longer adverbial phrases come at the end of a clause.
   I play tennis with Abi **once a week**.

2.4 Modals of possibility

We use *must, could, might* and *can't* + infinitive to speculate about a situation.

1 Use *must* + infinitive when you are sure that something is correct.
   You haven't eaten all day. You **must be** *hungry!*
   John hasn't arrived yet. He **must be** *stuck in traffic.*
2 Use *could* or *might* + infinitive when something is possible.
   The man in the photo **could be** *American, he has a big hat.*
   The book **might be** *on the table.*
3 Use *can't* + infinitive when something is impossible.
   You **can't be** *cold – it's 28 degrees out there!*

Unit 3

3.1 *-ing* form

When the *-ing* form of a verb is used like a noun, it is also called a gerund.

1 We use the *-ing* form when the verb is the subject or object of a sentence. We are usually talking about the action in a general way.
   Cycling *to work is healthier than* **driving**.
   Walking *home alone at night is a bad idea.*
2 We use *-ing* form after prepositions.
   I'm not happy **about working** *late.*
   Brian's nervous **about taking** *his driving test.*
3 We use the *-ing* form after certain verbs. These include *avoid, can't stand, consider, dislike, enjoy, finish, give up, imagine, involve, mind, practise, suggest, understand.*
   I can't stand **doing** *housework.*

3.2 Infinitives + *to*

An infinitive is the base form of the verb. It is usually preceded by *to*, but sometimes it is used without.

1 We use *to* + infinitive after adjectives.
   It's **difficult to climb** *Mount Everest.*
   I'm **pleased to meet** *you.*
2 We also use *to* + infinitive after certain verbs. *afford, agree, appear, arrange, ask, choose, decide, expect, hesitate, hope, learn, manage, offer, plan, promise, refuse, want.*
   We can't **afford to buy** *a new car.*
   Don't **hesitate to call** *if you need anything.*

3.3 Modals of obligation

We use *must, mustn't* and *have to* express strong obligation and necessity. We use *don't have to* to express lack of obligation.

1 We use *must* to talk about present and future strong obligations and necessities that come from the speaker.
   *I **must** tidy up my room later today.*

2 We use *mustn't* to tell people not to do things.
   *You **mustn't** tell her about the party – it's a surprise.*

3 We use *have to* to talk about strong obligations that don't come from the speaker.
   *You **have to** drive on the left in many countries.*

4 We use *don't have to* to talk about a lack of obligation in the present or in the future, to say that something is not necessary.
   *You **don't have to** come if you don't want to.*

5 We use *should* and *shouldn't* to give advice or talk about less strong obligation.
   *You **should** see a doctor about that cough.*
   *You **shouldn't** leave your computer screen on overnight.*

> **Watch Out!** After modal verbs (*must, mustn't, should, shouldn't*) or *make/let* someone do something, use the infinitive without *to*.

3.3 *make* and *let*

We can use *make* and *let* to express obligation.

1 We use *make + someone + do +* something to express the idea that someone caused you or forced you to do something.
   *My dad **made me laugh**.*
   *He **made me do** the washing-up.*

2 We use *let + someone + do +* something to express the idea of being allowed to do something.
   *The teacher **let me come** in late.*
   *They **let me have** more time.*

Unit 4

4.1 Past simple

USE   We use the past simple to talk about

1 an action that started and finished in the past.
   *We **went** to Florida for our holiday last year.*
   *I **saw** Jim yesterday.*

2 a situation in the past.
   *I **lived** in Japan for two years.*
   *Harry **was** really happy last week.*

FORM   Positive statements: subject + verb + *-ed*
   Negative statements: subject + *didn't* + infinitive
   Questions: *did* + subject + infinitive?

> **Watch Out!** There are many irregular verbs in the affirmative.

4.2 Present perfect simple

USE   We use the present perfect simple to talk about

1 an action that started and finished in the past but the time is indefinite (unknown or not important). We are usually talking about an action that happened at some time in our lives.
   ***Have** you ever **been** to New Zealand?*
   *I've **seen** this film.*

2 an action that started in the past but is not finished and is continuing now. We usually use *for* or *since. For* describes the length of the action. *Since* describes the starting point of the action.
   *Karen and Jeremy **have been** together **for** six months.*
   *We've **lived** here **since** 2000.*

3 repeated actions that have continued from a past time to the present time.
   *Belinda **has seen** several films recently.*
   *We've **been** to the gym six times this week.*

4 past actions with *ever, never, already, yet, just.*

   • We use *ever* and *never* to talk about 'at any time in your life'. *Ever* is usually used in questions. *Never* makes a statement negative. Both of them come before the main verb.
     *Have you **ever** sailed a boat?*
     *Jack has **never** learnt a second language.*

   • We use *already* to talk about an action that happened sooner than expected. It comes before the main verb.
     *I've **already** done the washing up.*

   • We use *yet* to talk about an action that we expect to happen. It is usually used in questions and negative sentences and comes at the end of the sentence.
     *I haven't spoken to Keith **yet**.*

   • We use *just* to talk about an action that happened a short time ago. It comes before the main verb.
     *Jeff has **just** found a £10 note.*

FORM   Positive statements: subject + *have/has* + past participle
   Negative statements: subject + *haven't/hasn't* + past participle
   Questions: *Have/Has* + subject + past participle?

4.3 *Used to* (past habits and states)

USE   We use *used to* to talk about past habits and states that don't occur now or no longer exist.
   *I **used to get** a new mobile every year but I wait a bit longer now.*
   *I **didn't use to be** able to talk in front of people but I'm more confident now.*
   *They **used to study** in this class, but they changed.*

FORM   Positive statements: *used to* + infinitive
   Negative statements: *didn't use to* + infinitive
   Questions: *Did you/she/they/*etc. + *use to* + infinitive?

Unit 5

5.1 Making comparisons

There are three types of comparison. We can compare things

1. to a higher degree (comparative form + *than*)
   *London is **colder than** Sydney.*
2. to the same degree (*as ... as*)
   *Los Angeles is **as warm as** Miami.*
3. to a lower degree (*less + than*)
   *Los Angeles is **less cloudy than** Glasgow.*

5.2 Comparative and superlative forms of adjectives and adverbs.

1. One-syllable adjectives
   - Add -*er* and -*est* to form the comparative and superlative forms.
     *The book was **longer than** the film.*
     *I'm the **fastest** writer in my class.*
   - With one-syllable adjectives that end in a vowel + consonant, double the consonant:
     big → bigger → biggest;
     sad → sadder → saddest
   - With one-syllable adjectives that end in -*e*, add -*r* and -*st*:
     safe → safer → safest
2. Two-syllable adjectives and adverbs:
   - With two-syllable adjectives ending in -*y*, replace the -*y* with -*i*:
     heavy → heavier → heaviest
   - Use *more* and *most* with two-syllable adjectives.
     *The city was **more modern** now.*
     *My sister is the **most careful** person I know.*
3. Three-syllable adjectives:
   - Use *more* and *most* with three-syllable adjectives or adverbs:
     *Jenny writes **more carefully** than I do.*
     *The president is the **most important** person in my country.*
4. Some comparative and superlative forms are irregular:
   good → better → best
   bad → worse → worst
   far → further → furthest
   *Spiderman 3 was **better** than Spiderman 2, but Spiderman 1 was the **best**.*
   *Martha's spelling is **worse** than David's, but mine is the **worst**.*
   *My job is **further** away than my brother's, but my dad's is the **furthest**.*

5.3 *too* and *enough*, *so* and *such*

USE

1. *Too* has the idea of excess or more than is necessary.
   *I'm **too tired** to go to the party.*
2. *Enough* means to the necessary degree.
   *I'm **fit enough** to run 20km.*
3. Use *so* and *such* with the meaning of *very*.
   *The gift was **so thoughtful**.*
   *He's **such a special person**.*
4. Often *too* and *enough* express contrasting ideas.
   *It **was too heavy** to carry.*
   *It **wasn't light enough** to carry.*
   *The box **was too big** to send by post.*
   *The box **wasn't small enough** to send by post.*

FORM

1. We use *too* before an adjective. Use *to + infinitive* to express result.
   *The weather was **too cold**.*
   *The weather was **too cold to go** out.*
2. We use *enough* after the adjective. Use *enough + infinitive* to express result.
   *It wasn't **warm enough**.*
   *It wasn't **warm enough to eat** outside.*
3. We can use *so + adjective* to replace *very* + adjective. Use *that* + clause to express result.
   *Her new boyfriend was **so kind**.*
   *Her new boyfriend was **so kind that** he drove us all to the station.*
4. We can use *such + a/an + adjective + noun* in place of *so + adjective*.
   *The party was **so great**.*
   *It was **such a great party**.*
   - for countable, singular nouns, use *such + a/an + adjective + noun*. Use *that* + clause to express result.
     *It was **such a great day**.*
     *She was **such a difficult person** that I never want to see her again.*
   - for uncountable and plural nouns, use *such + adjective + noun*. Use *that* + clause to express result.
     *It was **such terrible weather**.*
     *They were **such friendly people** that I wanted to go back.*

Unit 6

6.1 Past continuous

USE We use the past continuous

1. to talk about an action that was in progress when another past action happened.
I **was cleaning** the cupboard when I saw a mouse.
Peter cut his finger while he **was chopping** vegetables.

2. to talk about two past actions in progress at the same time.
I **was reading** a book while Bob **was cooking** dinner.
As the football team **were walking** into the stadium, people **were cheering**.

3. to talk about a past temporary action.
We **were working** in Leeds for the week.
I **was learning** to play the piano.

FORM Positive statements: subject + was/were + -ing form
Negative statements: subject + wasn't/weren't + -ing form
Questions: was/were + subject + -ing form

6.2 Past perfect simple

USE

- We use the past perfect simple to talk about a past action that happened before another past action.
I watched the film because I**'d enjoyed** reading the book.

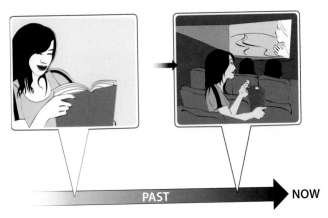

- We often use the past perfect simple with time expressions by the time, before and after.
By the time we arrived, the party **had finished**.
Before I took the exam, I**'d studied** a lot.
Kate called me after she**'d arrived** at the airport.

FORM Positive statements: subject + had + past participle
Negative statements: subject + hadn't + past participle
Questions: had + subject + past participle

Unit 7

7.1 Countable and uncountable nouns

1. Countable nouns can be used with
   - a singular or plural verb.
     The **boat is** in the harbour.
     The **people were travelling** abroad.
   - a/an for singular sentences.
     There's **a pool** and **an open theatre**.
   - some for plural positive sentences and questions.
     I had **some tickets** for that concert.
   - any for plural negative sentences and questions.
     They haven't got **any guests** at the moment.
     Are there **any biscuits** left?

2. Uncountable nouns
   - always use a singular verb.
     Information is valuable.
   - never use a/an.
     I hate it when there's **traffic** around.
   - can use some for positive sentences.
     He gave me **some advice**.
   - can use any for negative sentences and questions.
     There isn't **any rice** in the cupboard.
     Did you see **any ice** in the water?

> **Watch Out!** Some nouns have both countable and uncountable uses, e.g.
> glass (material) / a glass (drinking cup)
> coffee (the liquid) / a coffee (a cup of coffee)
> paper (material) / a paper (newspaper)
> noise (general) / a noise (specific)
> painting (general) / a painting (specific)

7.2 Quantifiers

1. Countable nouns
   - can use a lot of for positive sentences.
     There **are a lot of students** here.
   - can use many for negative sentences and questions.
     There **aren't many visitors** today.
     Are there many books left?
   - can use a few.
     There **are a few new ideas** here.

2. Uncountable nouns
   - can use a lot of for positive sentences.
     There's **a lot of water** here.
   - can use much for negative sentences and questions.
     There **isn't much bread** at home.
     Is there much time left?
   - can use a bit.
     There's **a bit of cake** in the fridge.

7.3 Articles

1 We use the indefinite article, *a/an*

- before single countable nouns that we are talking about for the first time.
  *I've bought **a new MP3 player**.*
  *Have you got **a key**?*
- before a noun that is one of many.
  *Is there **a bus stop** near here?*
  *I need **a glass** of water.*
- with jobs.
  *I'm **a teacher**.*
  *My sister's **an engineer**.*

2 We use the definite article, *the*

- for single countable nouns that we have talked about before.
  *We hired a car for a few days when our car was in the garage. After two hours, **the car** broke down!*
  *I bought a T-shirt from the supermarket for just £5. But when I put **the T-shirt** on, I realised it had a big hole in it.*
- with uncountable nouns or plural nouns when we are talking about a specific object or group.
  ***The children** played in the park.*
  *Could you pass **the salt**, please?*
- when there is only one of something.
  *Look at **the moon**.*
  *I'm going to **the train station**.*

3 We use no article with

- uncountable and abstract nouns.
  ***Do you want** sugar **in your** coffee?*
  *Life **isn't always fair**.*
- plural nouns when we talk about something in general.
  *Dogs **make wonderful** pets.*
  *Bananas **are good for you**.*
- most streets, towns, cities, countries, continents, language and names.
  *We lived in **Tokyo** in **Japan** and speak **Japanese**.*
  *I've travelled across **Europe**.*
  *Let's go shopping on **Oxford Street**.*
  *Where's **John**?*

> **Watch Out!** A few countries use *the*, including *the USA*, *the UK* and *the UAE*.

Unit 8

8.1 Reported speech

USE

1 We use **direct speech** when we report the exact words that someone says or writes.
'This is the best food I've ever eaten!' she said.
'We want more!' they all said.

2 We use **reported speech** when we report something that has been said or written. We don't use their exact words.
She said it was the best food she'd ever eaten.
They said that they wanted more.

FORM

- With direct speech, the words that are spoken sit between speech marks (' or ").
  'I've never been here before,' he said.
  They all shouted, 'Hurry up!'
  'I'm sorry,' she said, 'but I've broken your glass.'
- With reported statements, the form is as follows:
  verb (+ *that*) + clause
  We can use *say* and *tell* (and other verbs) to report statements. When we use *say*, we do not need an object. When we use *tell*, we need an object (you have to tell *someone*).
  She told me (that) she felt ill.
  He told us (that) he'd lost his wallet.
  They said (that) they wanted to go home.
  You said (that) you loved me.
- The verb form usually changes as follows:

direct speech	reported speech
present simple/continuous	past simple/continuous
*'I usually **get up** at 6am', he said.*	*He said he usually **got up** at 6am.*
'I'm reading a great book,' she said.	*She said she **was reading** a great book.*
past simple	past perfect simple
*'We **played** tennis together <u>yesterday</u>,' she said.*	*She said they'**d played** tennis together <u>the day before</u>.*
present perfect simple	past perfect simple
*'I'**ve lived** in this area for years,' Ben said.*	*Ben said he'**d lived** in this area for years.*
will	would
*'It'**ll rain** <u>tomorrow</u>,' said the weather forecaster.*	*The weather forecaster said it **would rain** <u>the next day</u>.*
can	could
*'I **can't sing** very well,' he said.*	*He said he **couldn't sing** very well.*

8.2 Reported questions

With reported questions, the form is as follows:

Wh- questions	
direct speech	reported speech
question word + auxiliary verb + subject + verb '**What are you doing?**' she asked.	question word + subject + verb She **asked** us **what we were doing**.

Yes/No questions	
direct speech	reported speech
auxiliary verb + subject + verb '**Do you want** a sandwich?' he asked.	if (or whether) + subject + verb He **asked** me **if/whether I wanted** a sandwich.

Unit 9

9.1 *look/look like*

We use *look* and *look like* to talk about similarity.

1. We use *look* with an adjective.
   He **looks tired**.
   This painting **looks very unusual**.

2. We use *look like* with a noun/adjective + noun.
   He **looks like a postman**.
   She **looks like a kind person**.

9.2 Modals of ability

USE   We use *can*, *could* and *be able to* to talk about ability.

1. We use *can* to talk about present and future ability.
   I **can play** the guitar.
   We **can paint** the bedroom tomorrow.

2. We use *could* to talk about general past ability.
   Steve **could run** fast when I was young.
   Al **couldn't read** very well until he was 9.

3. We use *be able to* to talk about present ability or future ability.
   She'**s** not **able to come** to the meeting.
   I'll **be able to call** you tonight.

4. We use *was/were able to* to say that someone managed to do something on one occasion. We cannot use *could* in this situation.
   We **were able to move** the wardrobe.
   They **were able to repair** the car.

Watch Out! *Could* and *can* are also used for requests.

FORM   subject + *can* + infinitive
subject + *could* + infinitive
subject + *am/is/are able to* + infinitive
subject + *was/were able to* + infinitive

9.3 Relative pronouns

The most common relative pronouns are

who: to refer to people.

which: to refer to things.

that: to refer to either people or things.

whose: the possessive of *who* and *which*.

when: after nouns referring to time.

where: after nouns referring to place.

Watch Out! *Whom* is very formal these days. It is used to refer to people as the object of a clause.

9.4 Relative clauses

1. Defining relative clauses
   - We use defining relative clauses to define or identify a noun. They are necessary to understand exactly which person, thing, time or place we are talking about.
     I gave the book to the student **who is sitting** next to the door.
     This is the key for the car **which is parked** outside.
   - Relative clauses always refer to the noun which comes immediately before.
     The **man who is wearing** a black jacket is friends with that girl.
     The man is friends with that **girl who is wearing** a black jacket.
   - No commas are used.
   - We can use *that* to refer to things. *That* can also be used in informal speech to refer to people.
     It's the book **that** I left on the table.
     Did you speak to the girl **that** was sitting over there?

2. Non-defining relative clauses
   - We use non-defining relative clauses to give extra information. They tell us more about a person, thing, time or a place that is already identified.
     Mr Cooper, **who** is meeting you next week, wants to know if the hotel is booked.
   - Commas are used before and after the relative clause.
   - We use *which* if a place is the subject of the relative clause.
     New York, **which is** no longer the world's largest city, is one of the most famous.
   - We use *where* if a place is the object of the relative clause.
     Buenos Aires, **where I lived** for three years, is a top tourist destination.
   - We don't usually use *that* in non-defining relative clauses.

Unit 10

10.1 Passive voice

USE   The passive is used to talk about processes, actions and events:

- when the process is more important than the person who did it (the agent),
- when we don't know who did it.

  The coffee beans are dried in a large, open room.

  The story was sold to the newspapers.

  We can include the 'agent' (i.e. who did it) in a passive sentence if it adds extra interesting information. We usually include it at the end of the sentence using *by*

  *This dress was worn **by Lady Gaga**.*

  ~~This dress was worn by someone.~~

  *This song was written **by Michael Jackson**.*

  ~~This song was written by someone.~~

FORM   We use the appropriate tense of *be* + past participle

- Present simple:

  *Thousands of things **are bought** online each day.*

- Present continuous:

  *My car **is being repaired** at the moment.*

- Present perfect:

  *My mobile **has been stolen**.*

- Past simple:

  *This website **was designed** by a teenager.*

- Past perfect:

  *The ring **had been lost** for years before they found it.*

10.2 get/have something done

USE

- We use *get/have something done* to say that somebody else did something for us. This is usually because you asked them to and often means that you paid for it.

  *I'm going to **have my watch repaired** at the jewellery shop.*

  *Henrietta **had her teeth checked** at the dentist this morning and they're all fine.*

  *The carpet's looking dirty. Let's **get it cleaned**.*

- Sometimes it can mean that you didn't want it to happen.

  *Evan **had his wallet stolen** at the supermarket yesterday.*

- *Have something done* is more common than *get something done*. *Get something done* is more informal.

FORM   *get/have* + object + past participle

Unit 11

11.1 Phrasal verbs

A phrasal verb is a verb with an adverb or preposition after it. These particles can be prepositions or adverbs. A phrasal verb usually has a different meaning than when the verb stands alone. There are four types of phrasal verb

1   Intransitive. These phrasal verbs need no object.

   *The plane **took off** at 6 a.m.*

   *The washing machine **broke down** yesterday.*

2   Transitive and separable. These need an object. The object can sit between the verb and particle.

   *I **turned** the light **on**. / I **turned on** the light.* (Both are acceptable)

   *My dad **picked** my shoes **up** from the floor. / My dad **picked up** my shoes from the floor.*

> **Watch Out!** When the object is a pronoun, it must sit between the verb and particle.
>
> *My dad **picked** me **up** from the station.* ~~My dad picked up me from the station.~~

3   Transitive and inseparable. These need an object. The object can only come after both the verb and particle. It cannot sit between the verb and particle.

   *Our neighbour sometimes **looks after** our daughter.* ~~Our neighbour sometimes looks our daughter after~~.

   I have to look for my glasses again. ~~I have to look for my glasses again~~.

4   Transitive and inseparable with two particles. These phrasal verbs need an object and have two particles. The object cannot go between the verb and particles.

   *I'm **looking forward to** meeting your parents.* ~~I'm looking your parents forward to meeting~~.

   *We **get on with** each other.* ~~We get on each other with~~.

11.2 Future forms

1   Present continuous

   We use the present continuous to talk about future arrangements. These are things which have already been decided.

   *I'm **meeting** Bill for coffee in an hour.*

   *We're **eating out** with Mary and Steve tomorrow evening.* (the date is in your diary, the restaurant is booked and your friends know what time to meet you)

FORM   subject + *am/is/are* + *-ing* form

2   *be going to*

   be going to is used to talk about plans and intentions. The decision has been made before the time of speaking but it has not yet been arranged.

   *Andy's **going to move** house next year.*

   *They're **going to visit** us sometime next month.*

FORM   subject + *am/is/are (not) going to* + infinitive

> **Watch Out!** We can also use *going to* to talk about predictions. See Grammar reference 11.3.

3 *will*

We use *will* for predicting something that we know or believe something about.

*I think Brazil **will win** the next World Cup.* (I know they're a good team)

*The lesson **will be** fun tonight.* (I know that lessons are usually fun)

FORM   subject + *will/won't* + infinitive

> **Watch Out!** We can also use *will* to talk about decisions. See Grammar reference 11.3.

4 Present simple

We use the present simple to talk about timetables and programmes.

*The bus **leaves** at 6.15 p.m.*

*The lesson **starts** at 8 p.m.*

11.3 *will* and *going to*

1 We can use both *will* and *be going to* to talk about predictions.

- We use *will* when we talk about predictions which are based on what we know or believe about something.

  *I'm sure she'**ll be** late again.* (I know that she's often late)

  *I think you'**ll do** really well in the exam.* (I believe you know the exam subject well)

- We use *be going to* when we talk about predictions based on good evidence that we can see, feel or hear now.

  *You'**re going to sleep** well tonight.* (I can see that you're very tired now)

  *It's **going to rain** in a minute.* (The sky's gone dark)

2 We use both *will* and *be going to* to tell people about decisions we make.

- We use *will* when we tell someone about a decision we make at the moment of speaking. These are decisions which are sudden.

  *[Phone rings] I'**ll get** it!*

  *I don't know what to do tonight. I'**ll** probably **watch** a film.*

- We use *be going to* when we tell someone a decision that has already been made. The decisions have become our plans and intentions.

  *We'**re going to move** house next year.*

  *I'**m going to study** really hard next week.*

Unit 12

12.1 Zero and first conditionals

USE   We use the zero conditional to talk about things that are always true.

*If my baby **is** thirsty, he **cries**.*

*If I **see** a spider, I **scream**!*

We use the first conditional to talk about things that might happen in the future, i.e. future possibility.

*If it's sunny tomorrow, we'**ll go** to the park.*

*If you **don't practise** hard, you **won't improve**.*

FORM   zero conditional: *If* + subject + present simple, subject + present simple (main clause)

first conditional: *If* + subject + present simple, subject + *will* + infinitive (main clause)

The *if* clause can go at the beginning or end of a sentence. When the *if* clause comes at the beginning, there must be a comma between the two clauses. When it comes at the end, no comma is needed.

*If the shop's open, I'**ll** buy you some chocolate.*

*I'**ll** buy you some chocolate if the shop's open.*

12.2 Second conditional

USE   We use the second conditional to talk about:

1 present or future situations that are unreal, untrue, or imagined.

*If she **were** taller, she **would be** a model.*

*If they **travelled** by train, they **could arrive** earlier.* (*could* = would be able to)

*He'**d get** fewer injuries if he **played** tennis instead of football.*

2 present or future situations we think they are impossible or unlikely to happen.

*If I **had** enough money, I'**d buy** that car.*

*If we **went** to India, we'**d visit** the Taj Mahal.*

*We **might do** more exercise if we **had** the time.* (*might* = would possibly)

FORM   *If* + subject + past simple, subject + *would/could/ might* + infinitive

The *if* clause (+ past simple) can go at the beginning or end of a sentence. When the *if* clause comes at the beginning, there must be a comma between the two clauses. When it comes at the end, no comma is needed.

> **Watch Out!** In the *If* clause, we can use both *was* and *were* after *I/he/she/it* but in formal situations, it is more usual to use *were*.

Writing reference

Contents

Improving your writing

1	What is a sentence?	p.134
2	Paragraphing your writing	p.135
3	Spelling	p.137
4	Planning your writing	p.139
5	Making your writing interesting	p.141
6	Editing your work	p.143
7	Punctuation	p.145
8	Getting the right tone	p.147

Exam task types

1	Transactional emails, postcards and notes	p.149
2	Informal letters	p.150
3	Stories	p.151

Improving your writing

1 What is a sentence? (Language)

1 All sentences must have a SUBJECT + VERB (+OBJECT)

subject	verb	object
Jack	arrived.	
She	wrote	her phone number.
My boss	rang	me.
I	didn't see	the problem.

We can call this basic structure SVO.

2 You can add adverbs, adjectives, place, time, etc. to the basic SVO sentence.

For example:

- *Jack arrived at the airport **on time**.*
- *She quickly left her phone number **on a piece of paper**.*
- *My boss rang me **at home yesterday morning**.*
- *I didn't see the problem **at first**.*

3 You can join two SVO sentences using conjunctions like *and, so, or, but*, etc.

1 When we join two SVO sentences with a conjunction, we call each SVO a 'clause'.
2 You don't need to use commas with these words.
3 With *and, or* and *but*, you don't need to repeat the subject or modals after these words.

For example:

- *She quickly wrote her phone number on a piece of paper **and** she passed it to me.*
- *We could go to the cinema **or** we could get a DVD to rent at home.*
- *I've had a very busy day **so** I'd rather stay at home.*
- *I love Italian food **but** my family all prefer the Spanish restaurant.*

4 You can also link two SVO sentences using conjunctions like *because, although, after, if* and *when*.

1 You can write the conjunction in the middle or at the beginning of the sentence.
2 If you write the conjunction at the beginning, you need a comma between the two clauses.
3 You need to use a pronoun (*he, she, it*) if you want to repeat a subject. Notice the punctuation and the use of pronouns in the examples below.

For example:

- *I love eating junk food, **although** I know it's unhealthy.*
- ***Although** I know junk food is unhealthy, I love eating junk food.*
- ***Because** the train was late, I missed the meeting.*
- *I left early **so** I wouldn't miss the start of the film.*

Practice 1

Five of the sentences are incorrect. Correct the mistakes.

1 We took the bus. Because the car was at the garage.
2 I was worried about his feelings so didn't tell the truth.
3 The film was really terrible, I left.
4 I wanted to buy a gift or send some flowers.
5 There are a lot of nice restaurants. And the sports centres are great in my town.
6 She texted when she was leaving.
7 After I read the letter I felt really sad.
8 When I get back home.

Practice 2

Join these ideas together to make longer sentences. Can you add an adjective, adverb, place or time to them?

1 Sue phoned Ian. It was Ian's birthday.
2 I lost my umbrella. I went to look for it.
3 I'd love to take you round the sights. I'd love to show you the local art gallery.
4 I left work early. I was late for the party.

2 Paragraphing your writing (Organisation)

1 What is a paragraph?

Successful paragraphing is essential to good writing. A paragraph is a part of a piece of writing which starts on a new line. It should contain more than one sentence. All sentences must be organised together by a topic or theme.

A paragraph usually starts with a topic sentence which makes the theme of the paragraph clear (see the highlighted sentence in the example below). For example:

There are lots of great places to visit near my house.
There's a dry ski centre where we can practise skiing and snowboarding, and there's a really nice mountain café nearby. My favourite place is the old castle. It's old and falling down these days, but in the summer they have concerts in the gardens.
I think it would be easier if I came to get you. I can get my brother to drive to the airport and he can help with the luggage. We're only about half an hour from the airport, but it's quite a difficult route.

Practice

Match these topic sentences to the correct paragraph.

A So when I went to the shops, it all became clear.

B I had no idea what to do next.

C I hadn't heard from Josie for years.

An old friend

(1) .... We'd been at school together from the age of about four. But when we both left school and went to different universities, we lost contact.

(2) .... It was a Saturday afternoon and I was trying on some new shoes for a party that evening.

'Liz!' She sounded frightened as she spoke. 'I need your help,' she said quickly. Then she hung up, without giving me the details of where she was or what she was doing.

(3) .... I walked down to the newsagents', and bought a newspaper. When I looked at the front page, I almost dropped the paper. The headline said, 'Local Girl Lost on Mount Everest,' and there was a photograph of my old friend Josie underneath.

2 Linking sentences in a paragraph

You should find connections between the sentences in your paragraph.

1 Use pronouns like *he, they, them, there*. For example:

Jake was the coolest guy in class. **He** was always invited to the best parties.
*I loved **my** school. I was really happy **there***.

2 Use linking words and expressions like *then, anyway, so*. For example:

*By the time I got home, I was wet and freezing cold. **Anyway**, it was a pretty bad day from start to finish.*

3 Use synonyms and paraphrases. For example:

*I've always loved **basketball**. It's the most exciting **game** ever invented.*

3 Linking paragraphs

In a letter, story or other long piece of writing (around 100 words), try to link paragraphs to show a development of ideas.

1 Use a linking word or phrase.

2 Repeat a word (or words) from the last sentence of one paragraph in the first sentence of the next paragraph.

3 Use a synonym or paraphrase.

For example:

We didn't know where to go. We managed to climb up the mountain just in time to see the ³wind lift one of our tents and blow it across the other side of the valley. We found a cave, with dry wood inside. We were soon dry and warm, and thankful that we were out of the worst.

¹The sun went down as we sat ²around the fire.

¹The following day we looked ²around the mess that ³the storm had left behind. We had lost most of the food and spare clothes that we'd brought with us, but we still had our mobile phones to be able to call for help.

Practice

Begin this paragraph with an appropriate topic sentence (A–C). Then complete spaces 1–8 with possible linking words or phrases.

(A) .... We started by going to all the typical tourist sites - the Empire State Building and Broadway. We took the ferry across the harbour to the Statue of Liberty.
(1) .... was a lot smaller than I thought it would be,
(2) .... we had a great time. We were so tired
(3) .... we got back to the hotel.
(B) .... My uncle lived in New York, so he was familiar with some of the less famous places.
(4) .... took us to a beautiful part of Central Park,
(5) .... we had lunch and watched the street entertainment. (6) .... he showed us a place where we could buy cheap tickets for the theatre that night. We were able to get seats at the musical Chicago. I loved the
(7) .... and the (8) ....
(C) .... I'm sure you would love to visit. Perhaps we can meet there together one day? Let me know about your holiday in your next letter.
Take care,
Mike

3 Spelling (Language)

1 Adding syllables

1 doubling the final consonant

We often double the final consonant in one-syllable words if they end in one vowel followed by one consonant, e.g. *shop* → *shop**ping***, *big* → *big**ger***, *stop* → *stop**ped***.

2 words ending in -e and -ee

We usually drop the final -e in words when the endings -ing or -ous are added, e.g. *writ**e*** → *writ**ing***, *fam**e*** → *fam**ous***,

The final e is not dropped from words ending in -ee, e.g. *s**ee*** → *s**eeing***, *agr**ee*** → *agr**eement***.

3 words ending in -y and -ie

We usually change y to i before -er or -ed, e.g. *angry* → *angr**ier***, *try* → *tr**ied***.
We do not change -y to -i before -ing, e.g. *try* → *try**ing***, *cry* → *cry**ing***.
We usually change -ie to -y before -ing, e.g. *lie* → *l**ying***, *die* → *d**ying***.

2 Adding -s

1 We often make the plural of nouns by adding -s, e.g. *boy* → *boy**s***, *cheese* → *cheese**s***.
2 We add -s to most verbs in the present simple for *he*, *she* or *it*, e.g. *like* → *like**s***, *buy* → *buy**s***.
3 However, we add -es after words which end in -o, -s, -ss, -sh, -ch and -x, e.g. *go* → *go**es***, *bus* → *bus**es***, *kiss* → *kiss**es***, *wish* → *wish**es***, *teach* → *teach**es***, *box* → *box**es***.

3 Irregular plurals

Below are some irregular plurals:

baby → *bab**ies***; *child* → *child**ren***; *knife* → *kni**ves***; *man* → *m**e**n*; *a person* → ***people***;
tooth → *t**ee**th*; *woman* → *wom**e**n*

4 Spelling and pronunciation

1 Homophones

These are words which are pronounced the same but spelled differently, e.g.

to → *too* → *two*; *there* → *they're* → *their*; *by* → *bye* → *buy*; *witch* → *which*; *here* → *hear*;
meat → *meet*; *peace* → *piece*; *plane* → *plain*; *war* → *wore*

Practice

Complete the sentences with the correct spelling.

1 (*to, too, two*)

  A I had .... slices of cake, it was so nice.

  B I love horror films, but I like comedies ....

  C I'm going .... see Chris later today.

2 (*there, they're, their*)

  A I saw Jim and Sarah at the weekend. .... moving house soon.

  B .... are a lot of things to do at night in my home town.

  C I love Frankie's restaurant, ... spaghetti bolognese is the best in town.

3 (*which, witch*)

  A I really didn't know .... way to go.

  B My little sister's dressing up as a .... for the school play.

4 (*here, hear*)

  A I .... that Bethany's back from her trip abroad!

  B I left the book right ....

5 (*meat, meet*)

  A I was planning to .... Jack later.

  B I think .... is an important part of a healthy diet.

---

2 Silent letters

These are words where a letter is written but not pronounced, e.g. *chocolate*; *business*; *different*; *vegetable*

Practice

Underline the silent letter in these words.

restaurant   comfortable   knife   interesting   Wednesday   answer
island   climb   psychology   calm

---

5 Improving your spelling

1 Use a dictionary.

A good dictionary can give you information about spelling a word, including any likely problems caused by adding *-ing* or *-ed* to the word. If you're not sure about the spelling of a word, check it in your dictionary.

drip[1] /drɪp/ *v* [I,T] (**dripped**, **dripping**) to let liquid fall in small drops: *That tap's still dripping.* | *Don't drip blood on the carpet!* | **[+from/off/through etc]** *Water was dripping through the ceiling.* | **be dripping with water/sweat etc** *They were both dripping with sweat.*

2 Keep a personal spelling list.

Write down words that you spell incorrectly. Add to your list each time you receive a piece of work back from a teacher with corrections. Revise your list regularly until you know how to spell that word.

3 Keep a vocabulary notebook with new words.

You are more likely to learn the correct spelling if you write the words down. When you see a new word, copy it into your notebook, then check that you have spelled it correctly. Revise it regularly.

4 Planning your writing (Content and Organisation)

Follow these stages before you write to make sure that you answer the question and get a higher grade for Content in the *Cambridge English: Preliminary* Writing Paper.

1 Think of ideas

You will need to think of as many ideas, words and phrases connected with the topic as you can think of. Here are some ideas for doing this successfully.

1 Don't worry about which ideas or phrases are better than the others. Write anything that you can think of.

2 Don't waste time writing complete sentences. Write words, draw symbols or put phrases down on the page.

2 Select and choose the best ideas

Choose the best ideas and tick (✓) them. In the exam you have a short word limit so only choose the best.

1 Make sure that you have enough ideas to answer all parts of the question. For Writing Question 6 (the short note or email), write the numbers 1–3 next to the content points that you need to include to make sure that you have covered them.

2 Make sure that you have a range of vocabulary related to the topic.

3 Write a plan

If the piece of writing is about 100 words long, you will need to use three paragraphs.

1 Choose the subject of each paragraph.

2 Organise your ideas into the separate paragraphs. This will help to make sure that your work is organised and covers all the points and will help you avoid having to make long changes later.

Practice

First look at the first exam task and the student's paragraph plan. Then look at the second exam task and complete steps 1–3.

1 Brainstorm some words or phrases around this topic.
2 Make sure you have answered both questions.
3 Complete the paragraph plan.

Exam task 1

- Your Scottish penfriend has written to you.

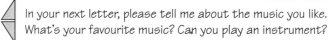

> In your next letter, please tell me about the music you like. What's your favourite music? Can you play an instrument?

- Now write a **letter** to your penfriend, answering his questions.
- Write your letter in about **100 words**.

---

essay plan	
paragraph theme	ideas
greeting	Dear Beth Thanks – good to hear. Sorry a bit slow to reply.
music	a) Music you can dance to – 80s disco! b) Played piano – school. Hated!
ending	What about you? Good to hear, etc. Best wishes

Exam task 2

- Your South African penfriend has written to you.

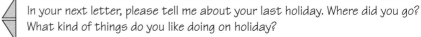

> In your next letter, please tell me about your last holiday. Where did you go? What kind of things do you like doing on holiday?

- Now write a **letter** to your penfriend, answering his questions.
- Write your letter in about **100 words**.

---

essay plan	
paragraph theme	ideas
greeting	
holidays	a) b)
ending	

5 Making your writing interesting (Content and organisation)

1 Introductions

In stories, a good introduction will explain the situation, use interesting vocabulary and introduce the people in the story. You should try to make the reader want to read more.

1 Start with direct speech.

For a dramatic start, begin with a piece of direct speech, e.g.

'Stop! Don't go in there!' he shouted.

'This, Miss Gonzales, is going to be a day you'll never forget,' the voice on the other end of the phone said calmly.

2 Start with the background information.

Start by explaining what was happening just before the main event, e.g.

I had been working on my university project all weekend.

Javier had been my closest friend for as long as I could remember. So when days and weeks passed without hearing from him, I knew something was very wrong.

2 Vocabulary

It is important that you use a good range of vocabulary. Try to think of better alternatives to words like *woman, good, like.*

For example:

*a **woman** → a stranger, a shop assistant, a well-dressed lady walking past*

*I **like** → I'd go for, I'm always keen on, I absolutely love*

***good**→ delicious, wonderful, comfortable, courageous, exciting*

Practice

Rewrite the story below with a better alternative to the words in bold.

> This is just a quick note to tell you that we arrived **okay**. The hotel is **nice**. The weather has been **bad**, but there's a **good** swimming pool. The food is **good** – I know you always **like** Greek food. Well, I have to go. Wish you were here.
>
> Matt

---

3 Mixed sentences

Try to use sentences with two clauses, as well as shorter sentences, e.g.

'So you Think you can Dance' is a popular TV show. It is the most popular in my country. It stars young dancers. People of all ages enjoy it.

'So you Think you can Dance' is the most popular TV show in my country. Although it stars young dancers, people of all ages enjoy it.

FOR MORE INFORMATION ON CLAUSES SEE PAGE 142.

Practice

Join the sentences to make one two-clause sentence using the word in brackets.

1 I was at your restaurant last week. I was not very pleased with the service. (*although*)
2 We were scared. We ran as fast as we could. (*so*)
3 I know you're going to love this group. They play the kind of music you always listen to. (*because*)
4 We turned the corner. We saw what was causing the noise. (*as soon as*)
5 I think you should bring a rain coat. It might be wet. (*in case*)

4 Adjectives and adverbs

Try to add adjectives and adverbs to your work to add interest or to show the mood.
For example:

~~I walked to the bus stop and waited.~~

I walked slowly to the bus stop in the freezing cold. I was feeling so lonely. I waited for what seemed like ages.

Practice

Add some adjectives or adverbs to make the sentences more interesting.

1 When we arrived at the town centre, we saw a man.
2 There's a mountain near a stream.
3 We walked up to the house and saw a lady at the window.
4 The streets were decorated and people were dancing to the music.
5 I would like to book a room for two nights.

5 Interesting verbs

Try to use all the verbs that you know in your writing, not the easy ones, e.g.

*I **broke** my glasses.* → *I **damaged** my glasses.*

*They **like** each other.* → *They **get along** well with each other.*

*He said he **wouldn't come**.* → *He **refused** to come.*

You will need to look at the construction of any new verbs in a dictionary before you start to use them.

refuse[1] /rɪˈfjuːz/ *v*
1 [I,T] to say firmly that you will not do or accept something: *I asked her to marry me, but she refused.* | **refuse to do sth** *Cindy refuses to go to school.* | **flatly refuse/refuse point blank (to do sth)** (=refuse completely) *Mother flatly refused to go back into hospital.* | *The offer seemed **too good to refuse**.*
2 [T] to not give or allow someone something that they want: **refuse sb sth** *we were refused permission to enter the country.*

Practice

Rewrite the sentences with a verb of similar meaning from the list. You may need to make other changes to the sentence. Use a dictionary to check the construction of any verbs you are unsure of.

forbid	fry	improve	knock down	refuse	slip	trust

0 *Bianca came and met us there.*
   Bianca joined us there.
1 I think my brother will do the right thing.
2 My granny fell on the ice last week.
3 I pushed the post with my car.
4 You need to cook the onions in a pan.
5 The owner of the shop said no to helping us.

6 Editing your work

It is important to check that you have written to the correct standard when you finish. Below are some of the things you should check for.

1 Content
- Have you done everything that you were asked to do in the question?
- Have you added a little expansion on each point?
- Have you written the correct number of words?

2 Communicative Achievement
- Have you thought about who you are writing to?
- Does your writing contain friendly phrases or a polite tone?
- Is your writing appropriately formal or informal?
- In a letter or email, have you started and finished with an appropriate phrase?

3 Organisation
- For pieces of writing of 100 words or more, have you written 2–4 paragraphs?
- Does each paragraph have a topic sentence?
- Is each sentence related to the topic of the paragraph?
- Are some of the sentences linked with linking expressions?
- Are some of the paragraphs linked with linking expressions?

4 Language
- Is there a good range of vocabulary?
- Do most of the sentences contain two clauses (SVOs)?
- Are the sentences varied with a good range of linking words?

Practice

Look at the task and student answer below. Has the student written to the correct standard? Use the checklist on page 143 to help you decide.

Exam task 1

Your penfriend from New Zealand has written to you.

> So how was that day out you were telling me about? Did you go? Was the weather alright? What did you do afterwards? I can't wait to hear.
> Zac

Now write to Zac answering his questions. Write about **100 words**.

Dear Josh

I went to a water park at the weekend. It was great. We got really wet, but the weather was warm, so it was alright. I went with my friend Maria Alejandra. She really loves that kind of thing. The slides were huge and really exciting, but I got sunburnt. I hope next time you're here to visit we can go together. You'd love the restaurant there and all the pools.

Yours sincerely

Sebastian

You will also need to check for errors. Below are some frequent errors you should check for.

1 Spellings, e.g. *I am **writting** to tell you…* → *I am **writing** to tell you…*
2 Use of tenses, e.g *I **go** there this weekend.* → ***I'm going** there this weekend.*
3 Style, e.g. ***I would like to recommend going** to the cinema tonight.* → ***Let's go** to the cinema tonight.*
4 Punctuation, e.g. *It was the **teachers** book.* → *It was the **teacher's** book.*
5 Incomplete sentences, e.g. ***When I arrived.*** → ***When I arrived,** the train was just leaving.*
6 Subject – verb agreement, e.g. *he **go*** → *he **goes***
7 Wrong word, e.g. *My brother **borrowed** me his book.* → *My brother **lent** me his book.*
8 Grammar, e.g. *I'm looking forward **to see** you later.* → *I'm looking forward **to seeing** you later.*
9 Word order, e.g. *It was a **day long**.* → *It was a **long day**.*
10 Articles, e.g. *I **am student**.* → *I am a student.*

Practice

There are ten errors in the student's work below. The first one has been corrected for you. Use the error checklist to help edit and improve the work.

> Hi Josh   *too formal*
> ~~I would like to thank you for your letter.~~ Thanks for
> your letter. It sounds like you had great time at your
> party.
> Well, I went to the water park. When we arrive it was
> really quite so we were able to go on everything. One of
> the slides was high a hundred meters. I went with my
> friend Gabriel — you know how much he love that kind
> of thing.
> When we left the water park. We were so tired that we
> decided not going to the cinema. We hired a movie and
> got a take away. I hope we can do it agin when your
> next here.
> Anyway, all the best,
> Andrea

7 Punctuation (Language)

1 Capital letters

We use capital letters:

1 at the beginning of a new sentence:
   e.g. ***We*** *had such a great time at your party!*
   Suddenly*, there was a terrible noise.*

2 for the names of particular things:
   people and titles e.g. *Catherine, The Times, the President*
   countries, towns and places, e.g. *Brazil, New York, South Africa, Broadway, New Street*
   nationalities and languages, e.g. *Argentinian, Spanish, Italian, English*
   days and months, e.g. *Friday, January, Independence Day*

2 Full stops (.), question marks (?) and exclamation marks (!)

We use full stops to end most sentences. We use question marks to end questions. We use exclamation marks to end sentences with a lot of emotion.

For example:

- *The books arrived on time.*
- *What would you like to do when you get here?*
- *Thank you for such a beautiful gift. I absolutely love it!*

3 Commas (,)

We use commas

1 after an introductory clause, e.g.

Nowadays, many people prefer to use the internet for shopping.

At first, I thought it was just the wind.

Suddenly, I was falling down the mountain!

After I left the road and entered the woods, I knew I'd made a mistake.

2 around added information, e.g.

I spent the summer in Sydney, which is the biggest city in Australia, and had a lovely time.

I spoke to your receptionist, Miss Jones.

3 between items on a list, e.g.

We were able to try surfing, kite boarding and sailing on the course.

4 to divide groups of words in a sentence to make the meaning clearer, e.g.

He told me that he wasn't a salesman, but that he was actually my long lost brother.

When we got there we had a cup of coffee, put the fire on, and sat down for a chat.

4 Apostrophes (')

We use apostrophes

1 when we use contractions, e.g. *I won't be able to meet you myself, but I'll send my brother.*

2 to show possession, e.g. *I met Dan's girlfriend at the party.*

5 Punctuation in direct speech

1 Direct speech always starts with a capital letter, e.g.

The boy screamed, 'Don't touch it!'

2 A comma (,) is usually used between the direct speech and the reporting phrase (*he said, Jack shouted*), e.g.

Jack bent down and said quietly, 'It's never going to happen.'

3 If the reporting phrase (*he said, Jack shouted*) comes after the direct speech, we usually put a comma before the final quotations marks, e.g.

'I hate you,' she said with tears in her eyes.

4 We use quotation marks when we repeat the exact words someone says (direct speech). Single quotation marks ('…') are more common in British English. Double quotation marks ("…") are more common in American English.

Practice

Read the story and write it again with the correct punctuation.

it all began with a telephone call one sunday morning I was just sitting down to read the times newspaper and enjoying a cup of coffee when the phone rang

is that miss abrahms asked the voice on the other end of the phone i didnt recognise the voice I thought it was probably one of those sales people

i have a special message for you from your long lost uncle frank he said I was going to put the phone down on him I didnt have an uncle frank that I knew of when he explained that he was a lawyer and was looking for frank jamesons only living relative three weeks later I was in the first class section of a plane to torronto to sign the papers that were going to make me so rich i would never need to work again

8 Getting the right tone

1 Formal or informal?

The tone of your language depends on

1 who you are writing to.

2 why you are writing.

You need to use an informal style to write to people you know as friends. You need to use a more formal style to write to someone you've never met, such as an enquiry about a hotel or a job application. Emails and letters can be either formal or informal

Below are some examples of formal and informal writing.

formal language	
examples	features
I would like to ask if you have any rooms available next week. *I am afraid that I have left my mobile phone at your offices.* *I was sad to learn that the centre was closed.*	Don't use contractions (*I would* instead of *I'd*) Use formal linking words (e.g. *however* instead of *but*) Use formal vocabulary (e.g. *available* instead of *free*) Use polite language even if you are complaining or criticising (e.g. *I was disappointed with the service* instead of *The service was rubbish*)
informal language	
examples	features
I've got a fantastic new job. You should see my new office! *Let me know what you think.* *Well, I have to go now, but get in touch soon.* *Don't you just love holidays?*	Use contractions (*I've been* instead of *I have been*) Address the reader personally (*You must be joking!* instead of *It sounds unlikely.*) Write plenty of questions (*How are you?* instead of *I am writing to ask about…*) Use strong adjectives and adverbs (*absolutely fantastic* instead of *quite pleasant*) Use informal vocabulary (*got* instead of *received*)

Practice

Look at the sentences below and decide if they have the features of formal (F) or informal (I) writing.

1 I'm so excited that you're coming to my country. It's going to be absolutely great!

2 I would like to collect the items at the end of the week, if that is convenient for you.

3 My main concern was the fact that the room was not very clean.

4 I would be grateful if you could tell me your decision as soon as possible.

5 What an amazing story! Well, you know, something similar happened to me.

6 I guess I'll have to go know. Someone has to keep up the good work!

2 Tone in letters

There are rules about starting and ending letters.

For formal letters, there are two options:

- If you don't know the name of the person you're writing to, start with *Dear Sir/Madam* and finish with *Yours faithfully.*
- If you do know the name, start with *Dear Mr Johnson/Dear Mrs Young* (never *Dear Mrs Anna*) and finish with *Yours sincerely* or *Kind regards.*

With informal letters or emails:

- start with *Hello Ben/Hi Ben* and finish with *Speak soon/Best wishes/Love.*
- We usually use *Love* when we're writing to close family or romantic partners. Women often use it when they write to close friends but men don't often do this.

Practice

Look at the extracts from an informal letter. Choose the better phrase.

Hi Cath

[1]It was so good to hear from you / I was pleased to receive your previous letter. It's always nice to get your news. Oh my goodness! [2]I would like to recommend the film 'Highlander'. / I can't believe you haven't seen the film 'Highlander' yet. You must go and see it. [3]I think you'll find it satisfactory. / You're going to love it.

…

Oh well, that's about all my news for now. [4]I can't wait to hear from you so write back soon. / I look forward to hearing from you.

[5]Lots of love / Yours sincerely,

Jane

FOR MORE INFORMATION ON INFORMAL LETTERS, SEE PAGE 150

Exam task types

Transactional emails, postcards and notes

(FOR MORE WORK ON TRANSACTIONAL EMAILS, POSTCARDS AND NOTES, SEE PAGES 31, 49, 93)

When you write a transactional email, postcard or note, it is very important to cover all the points that you have been asked to mention, using an appropriate tone.

EXAM TASK

You have just returned from a week's holiday staying with your British friend, Chris. Write an email to your friend thanking him for the visit.

In your card you should:

- Thank Chris for the visit
- Tell Chris what you enjoyed most about the visit
- Invite Chris to come and stay with you.

Write **35–45 words**.

Model answer

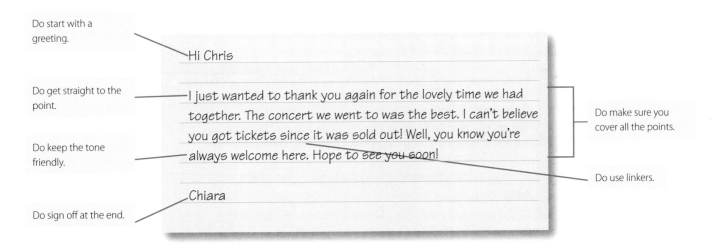

Do start with a greeting.

Hi Chris

Do get straight to the point.

I just wanted to thank you again for the lovely time we had together. The concert we went to was the best. I can't believe you got tickets since it was sold out! Well, you know you're always welcome here. Hope to see you soon!

Do keep the tone friendly.

Chiara

Do sign off at the end.

Do make sure you cover all the points.

Do use linkers.

Useful language

Openings
- Hi Steve
- Hope you're well.
- I just wanted to …
- Just a quick note to let you know that …

Keeping the right tone
- Well, …
- Anyway, …
- Hope to …
- You know …

Closings
- Write back soon!
- Hope it's good news!

Informal letters

(FOR MORE WORK ON INFORMAL LETTERS, SEE PAGES 13, 67, 103)

When you write an informal letter to a friend, it is important to use interesting language and use an appropriate tone.

EXAM TASK

This is part of a letter that you receive from a Scottish friend.

> I have to start learning another language for my business course at university. Which language do you think would be most useful? Do you have any advice to make learning a foreign language easier?

Now write a **letter** to your friend.
Write about **100 words**.

Model answer

Do start with a greeting. Create a name.

Do make reference to the letter that you've just received.

Do keep the tone friendly.

Do start a new paragraph when you start to answer a new question.

Do sign off at the end with your name.

Do finish the letter with an appropriate phrase.

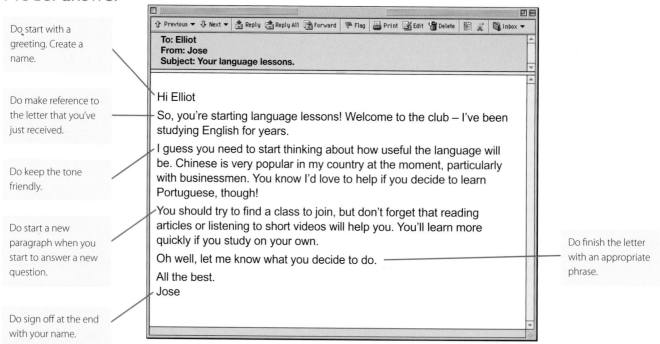

> Previous ▼ | Next ▼ | Reply | Reply All | Forward | Flag | Print | Edit | Delete | Inbox ▼
>
> **To:** Elliot
> **From:** Jose
> **Subject: Your language lessons.**
>
> Hi Elliot
>
> So, you're starting language lessons! Welcome to the club – I've been studying English for years.
>
> I guess you need to start thinking about how useful the language will be. Chinese is very popular in my country at the moment, particularly with businessmen. You know I'd love to help if you decide to learn Portuguese, though!
>
> You should try to find a class to join, but don't forget that reading articles or listening to short videos will help you. You'll learn more quickly if you study on your own.
>
> Oh well, let me know what you decide to do.
>
> All the best.
>
> Jose

Useful language

Openings
- It was great to hear from you again.
- Wow! I can't believe you're coming to visit.
- Sorry I'm a bit late replying – I've been so busy at uni.

Informal language
- I had a fantastic time.
- You are just going to love this, I know.

Making requests
- Do you think you could …
- Would you mind if we didn't …

Giving bad news
- I'm really sorry, but I'm not going to be able to …
- I'm afraid I've got some bad news. I haven't been able to …

Use linking words
- As I was saying earlier, …
- Anyway, I guess I need to tell you about …

Closing statements
- Let me know what you think.
- Get in touch soon. Don't be a stranger!

Stories

(FOR MORE WORK ON WRITING STORIES, SEE PAGES 21, 57, 75)

When you write a story, it is important to organise your ideas well, and use interesting language.

EXAM TASK

Your English teacher has asked you to write a story.

Your story must begin with this sentence:

Sam knew he had to leave immediately.

Write your **story** in about **100 words**.

Model answer

Do add a title.

Do say what happened just before, or what happened next.

Do make sure you use the correct punctuation in direct speech.

Do use a mixture of short and long sentences to make the story exciting.

Do use adjectives and interesting words.

Do use a good range of narrative tenses.

Don't start all your sentences 'Sam went, Sam thought, etc.'

The mysterious piano

Sam knew he had to leave immediately. The letter from his aunt in New York sounded urgent. She'd said something about a piano which didn't make sense. Sam boarded the plane, and eight hours later he was met by a strange man at JFK airport.

'Your aunt is sadly no longer with us,' he said in a cruel voice. Sam was shocked! 'Did she ever mention a key?' Sam panicked. He ran to the nearest police station. With their help, he went to his aunt's apartment. There, in the piano, was a strange pile of photos.

This is the key to putting a top criminal in prison,' said the police officer. Sam knew he'd made the right decision coming.

Useful language

Feelings
- Sam was frozen with fear.
- It was like a dream come true.

Direct speech
- 'Don't do anything stupid, now!'
- 'Hand over the money!'

Time linkers
- Suddenly, the lights went out.
- The next thing Sam knew, he was waking up in a strange room.
- By the time Sam realised what was happening, it was too late.
- When he got there, they'd already left.

Ending the story
- That was the last time Sam questioned his dad's advice.
- Sam looked at his friend and just laughed.

Functions bank

Speaking test

Giving personal information (Part 1)

1 Complete the sentences so they are true for you.

1 My name's .... It's spelt ....
2 I come from .... in ....
It's spelt ....
3 I live with ....
4 I'm a/an .... at ....
5 I'm learning English because ....
6 I think learning English is important because
....
7 On weekday mornings I ....
8 In the evenings I ....
9 At weekends I ....
10 Yesterday I ....
11 Last weekend I ....
12 Next weekend I ....

This table shows the English alphabet grouped by vowel sound. This can help you to spell your name and town/city well.

/eɪ/ e.g. make	/iː/ e.g. sheep	/e/ e.g. bed	/aɪ/ e.g. lie	/əʊ/ e.g. note	/uː/ e.g. boot	/aː/ e.g. father
a, h, j, k	b, c, d, e, g, p, t, v	f, l, m, n, s, x, z	i, y	o	q, u, w	r

Expressing likes, dislikes and preferences (Part 4)

2 Make the sentences true for you.

1 I absolutely love going to ....
2 I really like ....
3 I don't mind .... but I don't love it.
4 I'm not very keen on ....
5 I don't like .... very much.
6 I can't stand .... at all.
7 I prefer eating .... to ....

Paraphrasing when you don't know a word (Part 3)

3 Look at the photo. Imagine you are trying to describe the features in brackets from the photo, but don't know the words. Complete the sentences describing the features using words that you *do* know.

1 I don't know the name of the animal but it lives
.... (*squirrel*)
2 The animal is standing on something which looks like
.... (*rock*)
3 On the left of the photo there ....
(*forest*)
4 The couple are sitting in front of ....
(*lake*)

Saying where things are in a photo (Part 3)

4 Look at the photo. Match the first half of each sentence 1–8 with the second A–H.

1 In the foreground,
2 In the background in the middle,
3 Behind the animal there
4 All three of them
5 On the left of the photo,

A there's a forest.
B there's a squirrel looking at the camera.
C are in front of a beautiful lake.
D are two people sitting together.
E there are some mountains with snow on the top.

Asking for and making suggestions (Part 2)

5 **Put the verb in brackets in the correct form in each sentence.**

1 How about .... her some flowers? (*buy*)
2 What film do you think we .... ? (*watch*)
3 It'd be a good idea .... an umbrella. (*take*)
4 Why don't we .... the theatre trip? (*choose*)
5 What do you suggest .... ? (*do*)
6 We could .... water skiing. (*try*)

Discussing opinions (Parts 2 and 4)

6 **Put the headings in the correct place.**

Agreeing	Asking for someone's opinion
Disagreeing	Giving your opinion

1 ....
   I think football is a boring sport to watch.
   In my opinion, men are better drivers than women.
   If you ask me, people should stop spending so much.
   I feel strongly that we need to treat animals better.
   As I see it, it's more relaxing to have a beach holiday than a city break.

2 ....
   What do you think?
   Do you agree with me?
   I don't like it. What about you?
   What's your opinion about that?
   How do you see it?

3 ....
   Absolutely!
   You might be right.
   You've got a point there.
   I couldn't agree with you more.
   I agree with you.

4 ....
   Yeah, but what about the cost?
   You're joking!
   I don't think so.
   I can't agree with you about that.
   I don't agree with you.

7 **Look at the opinions in section 1 of Activity 6. Do you agree or disagree with them? Use phrases from sections 3 and 4.**

Managing a discussion (Parts 2 and 4)

8 **What do you say in each of these situations? Match situations 1–8 to phrases A–H.**

1 You didn't hear what someone said.
2 You didn't understand or you want to check what someone said.
3 You want to explain something more clearly.
4 You want to start a discussion.
5 You want to invite your partner to express his/her ideas.
6 You want to return to a previous topic.
7 Someone is talking a lot and you want to join in.
8 Your partner asks to join in the discussion.

A I'm not sure I know what you mean. / So, what you're saying is…
B Going back to (*the topic*)…
C Sorry, could you say that again? / Could you repeat that, please?
D Sorry, could I say something?
E What I mean is that… / What I want to say is that…
F Of course, go ahead.
G So, shall we talk about the first picture? / Let's discuss extreme sports.
H What do you think about that? / Can you tell me more about that?

Guessing information (Part 3)

9 **Complete the guesses about the photo on page 152 with a word from the list.**

seems	perhaps	looks like	might
probably	possible	look as if	look

1 They're .... a couple because they're sitting very close to each other.
2 It .... be autumn because the people are wearing jackets but there isn't much snow on the mountains.
3 The couple .... happy.
4 The squirrel .... to be interested in the camera.
5 I don't know where it is but it .... Canada.
6 .... the squirrel is wondering what the camera is.
7 It's .... that the squirrel wants to be famous!
8 It .... the couple is laughing at the squirrel.

Review (Parts 1, 2, 3, 4)

10 **What do you say in these situations in the Speaking test?**

1 You're asked to spell your name.
2 You're asked what you do in your free time.
3 You have to choose the best place for a holiday. You want to suggest the beach holiday to your partner.
4 You make the suggestion but your partner says nothing.
5 You're asked to describe a photo with a wardrobe in it but you can't remember the English word.
6 There's a person in the photo. Is he a policeman? You're not sure.
7 You want to give your opinion about the internet.
8 Your partner says he loves pasta because it's easy to cook.
9 Your partner asks you what films you like and don't like.
10 Your partner says he can't stand horror films because they're too scary.

Writing test (Parts 2 and 3)

Starting and finishing a letter/ an email

1 **Decide which phrases start and which phrases end a letter/an email.**

1 Best wishes,
2 Dear Sophie,
3 Hi John!
4 Love,
5 It was lovely to hear from you!
6 Anyway, I must go now. Write soon!
7 I was really pleased to get your letter/email.
8 I hope to hear from you soon.

Saying why you are writing

2 **Put the words in the correct order.**

1 about / writing / I'm / you / my weekend / to tell
2 my birthday party / asked / about / me / You
3 give you / some advice / You'd / to / like me
4 know / about / wanted / You / music / my favourite / to
5 some / writing / because / have / I / news / I'm
6 about / like / to tell / holiday / my last / I'd / you

Writing a story

3 **Decide if the phrases come at the beginning, middle or end of the story.**

1 Suddenly, there was a huge scream.
2 We all had a good laugh about it in the end.
3 One day, I was walking down the road when…
4 So, that's the reason why I never go to London.
5 Eventually, he said my name.
6 I'll always remember the time when…

Apologising, thanking, inviting

4 **Is each phrase 1–8 used to *apologise*, *thank*, *invite*, or *accept/reject an invitation*?**

1 Would you like to go to the cinema with me? *invite*
2 I'm afraid I've lost your camera. *apologise*
3 I'm afraid I can't go shopping with you on Saturday. *reject*
4 Thank you for your fantastic advice. *thank*
5 I'd like to invite you to my party on Thursday. *invite*
6 Thanks for sending me your new email address. *Thank*
7 I'd love to come! *accept*
8 I'm so sorry but I can't find your CD anywhere. *apologise*

Making suggestions

5 **Match the first half of each sentence 1–4 with the second A–D.**

1 Why don't we meet
2 How about
3 We could see
4 I think we should take

A a film tonight, if you like.
B a sightseeing tour of the city.
C at 6 p.m. outside the cinema?
D trying the new Chinese restaurant tomorrow?

Making offers and promises

6 **Complete the phrases with the correct words.**

shall	'll	won't	promise	would

1 .... you like me to bring anything?
2 .... I call you next week?
3 I .... I'll return it to you tomorrow.
4 I .... forget, I promise!
5 Don't worry! I .... come and meet you.

Responding to a letter/ an email

7 **Match the responses A–E to information received from friends in a letter/an email (1–5).**

1 'I failed my driving test and have to take it again.'
2 'We're going to have a baby!'
3 'I'm doing really well in my French class.'
4 'I've got a job interview on Tuesday.'
5 'Someone stole my phone with all my numbers in it.'

A It was great to hear your news! Congratulations!
B Good luck for next week!
C I'm sorry to hear that you didn't pass.
D What terrible news! I hope the police find it soon.
E I'm so happy to hear that things are going well.

Giving advice

8 **Complete the phrases with an appropriate word from the list.**

should	was/were	could	don't	idea

1 You .... try your local sports club.
2 Why .... you speak to your teacher?
3 I think it's a good .... to ask your boss.
4 If I .... you, I'd do a course in photography.
5 You .... tell your friend how you feel.

Expressing cause, effect and purpose (Parts 2 and 4)

9 **Decide whether the underlined part of each sentence is expressing something's *cause*, *effect* or *purpose*.**

1 I don't think we should choose this one <u>because it isn't pretty</u>.
2 It was raining <u>so we decided not to go out</u>.
3 <u>As it's fun to work with other people</u>, I prefer team sports.
4 I went to the beach <u>to learn how to surf</u>.
5 We need water <u>in order to live</u>, so we should use it carefully.
6 <u>Because she likes chocolates</u>, I think we should buy our teacher a big box of them.

10 **Complete the sentences to make them true for you.**

1 I'm taking English lessons because ....
2 I want to speak English well in order to ....
3 Because many people in the world speak Mandarin Chinese, ...
4 Learning a language is important so ....
5 Because there are a lot of English words to learn ....
6 To pronounce words correctly, ...

Exam focus

Paper 1: Reading and Writing
(1 hour 30 minutes)

Reading Part 1
(Three-option multiple choice)

What is being tested?

Part 1 tests your understanding of different short texts.

What do you have to do?

- Read five very short texts, e.g. notices, text messages, and three options (A–C) for each text.
- Choose the option that best matches the main message of the text.

Strategy

1 Read the instructions and look at the example.
2 Read the first text and think about where you might see it and who it is written for.
3 Try to decide what the main message is.
4 Read each option carefully and decide which one matches the main message.

Reading Part 2 (Matching)

What is being tested?

Part 2 tests your ability to read in detail.

What do you have to do?

- Read five descriptions of people (6–10) and eight short texts (A–H) on things like films, courses, books, etc.
- Match each person's needs to one of the eight texts. There will be three extra texts.

Strategy

1 Read the instructions and the text title to get the topic.
2 Read the descriptions of people carefully and underline the key words.
3 Scan each section of the main text to look for information that matches the descriptions. Look for words or phrases which are similar in meaning to the questions. Highlight possible answers.
4 Read the highlighted sections carefully to check which is an exact answer to the question. The correct answer will match *all* of the needs in the description.

Reading Part 3 (True/False)

What is being tested?

Part 3 tests your ability to find specific information.

What do you have to do?

- Read a text which gives information about something. It might come from an article, brochure, website or advert.
- Decide whether ten sentences (11–20) are correct (A) or incorrect (B). The questions follow the text order.

Strategy

1 Read the instructions and the text title to find the topic.
2 Quickly read all of the sentences to get an idea of what you have to look for.
3 Scan the text to find where the information is talked about. Look for words/phrases that mean the same as the key words you underlined in the sentences.
4 Read the section of the text carefully to check whether the sentence is true or false.

Reading Part 4
(Four-option multiple choice)

What is being tested?

Part 4 tests your understanding of the general meaning of a longer text and the writer's purpose, attitude or opinions.

What do you have to do?

- Read a longer text which expresses attitude or opinion.
- Answer five questions (21–25) about the text, each with four multiple-choice options (A–D).
- The first question asks about the writer's intention. The middle three questions ask about specific information in the text, and follow the order of the text. The fifth question asks about the general meaning of the text.

Strategy

1 Read the instructions and the text title to get the topic.
2 Skim the text to get an idea of what it is about. Then read the questions.
3 Read the text again and highlight the sections where you will find the answers to questions 22–24.
4 Reread these sections carefully and choose the correct answers. Don't match words in the text and options. Look for words and phrases that have the same meanings as the words in the text.
5 For questions 21 and 25, you think about the whole of the text. Try to answer without looking at the options and choose the best.

Reading Part 5
(Four-option multiple-choice cloze)

What is being tested?

Part 5 tests your knowledge of vocabulary, including words with similar meanings. It also tests some grammatical features such as articles, modal verbs and linking words.

What do you have to do?

- Read a short text with ten spaces in it.
- For each space, choose from four possible options.

Strategy

1 Read the title and the text quickly to get an idea of what it is about. Don't try to complete the spaces yet.
2 Read the text again. Stop at each space and try to predict what the missing word might be.
3 Look at the options for each space. Try putting each of the options in the space to see which one fits best.
4 Read the whole text again to make sure the options you have chosen make sense.

> **EXAM TIP**
>
> Leave any questions that you are not sure about; but go back and answer them at the end as you will not lose marks for a wrong answer. Choose the most likely answer.

Writing Part 1
(Sentence transformations)

What is being tested?

Part 1 tests a range of grammatical structures as well as vocabulary, and shows examiners that you can express yourself in different ways.

What do you have to do?

- Look at five pairs of sentences on the same topic.
- Complete the second sentence with up to three words so that it has the same meaning as the first sentence.

Strategy

1 Read the first sentence. Then read the second. Think about what is being tested, e.g. active to passive form.
2 Identify what is missing from the second sentence.
3 Write down the missing words. Make sure you have not written more than three words (contractions, e.g. *don't*, count as two words), or changed the meaning.
4 Check your spelling and that the sentences make sense.

Writing Part 2
(Short communicative message)

What is being tested?

Part 2 tests your ability to communicate a message clearly in an email or note. It involves giving advice, thanking, apologising, warning, inviting, etc.

What do you have to do?

- Write a short communicative message, for example a note, email or postcard.
- The instructions contain three points which you must include in your message.
- Write 35–45 words.

Strategy

See Writing Reference page 138

Writing Part 3
(Longer piece of continuous writing)

What is being tested?

In Part 3, you can choose to write either a letter or a story. The letter tests your ability to respond to news, describe something, give advice etc. The story tests your ability to organise ideas into a beginning, middle and end. Part 3 lets you show the examiner the range of language and structures that you know.

What do you have to do?

- Choose one of the two tasks you are given.
- *Letter:* you see part of a letter from an English-speaking friend and must write a suitable reply.
- *Story:* you are given either the title or the first line. Make sure your story follows on from this, or you will lose marks.
- Write an answer using appropriate format and style.
- Write around 100 words.

Strategy

See Writing Reference page 138

Paper 2: Listening (approx 30 minutes)

Part 1 (Multiple choice)

What is being tested?

Part 1 tests your ability to listen for specific information.

What do you have to do?

- Listen twice to seven short extracts (1–7) about different topics. These may be monologues (one person speaking) or dialogues (two people speaking).
- Each text has one question and three answers to choose from. Each option is represented by a picture.

Strategy

1 Read the questions and look at the pictures. Think about what is different about each set of pictures.
2 Mark the option that you think is best on your answer sheet.

Part 2 (Multiple choice)

What is being tested?

Part 2 tests your ability to listen for specific information.

What do you have to do?

- Listen to one monologue or an interview with a radio presenter. The main speaker(s) is usually giving information. You will hear the text twice.
- For each of the six questions (8–13), choose the correct option (A, B or C). The questions are in the same order as the information in the recording.

Strategy

1 Read the questions or sentence beginnings and then the options.
2 Mark the option that you think is best on your answer sheet.

Part 3 (Gap-fill)

What is being tested?

Part 3 tests your ability to listen for detail, specific information and opinion in a longer text. It's important to listen for and interpret information.

What do you have to do?

- Read the page of gapped notes about the recording.
- Listen twice to a speaker giving information about a particular topic.
- Complete the six gaps in the notes (14–19) with a word or words you hear in the recording.

Strategy

1 Read the notes. Underline key words and think about the kind of information that is missing.
2 As you listen, try to complete the gaps. The notes are in the same order as the information on the recording.
3 You will usually need to write one or two words in each gap. You should write exactly the words you hear; you do not need to change these words.
4 You might hear more than one word that could fill the gap. For example, if you need a price, you may hear three. Listen carefully and choose the correct one!
5 Check that your spelling of common words is correct and that the sentences make sense.

Part 4 (True/False)

What is being tested?

Part 4 tests your ability to understand the attitudes and opinions of speakers in an informal dialogue. You decide if six statements are true or false.

What do you have to do?

- Listen twice to an informal dialogue.
- Decide if the six statements (20–25) are true or false.

Strategy

1 Read the statements carefully. Underline key words, especially words of attitude and opinion (*was surprised by, was keen on*) and think about the kind of information you will hear (you are given some time for this).
2 As you listen, compare the statements to the opinions that the speakers express. The statements are in the same order as the opinions on the recording.
3 The correct answer is unlikely to use the same words as the statements. Listen for synonyms or words with the opposite meaning.

EXAM TIP

When you listen again, check your answers and complete any remaining sentences – you don't lose marks for a wrong answer. You will be given some time to read the questions and options *before* you listen.

Paper 3: Speaking (10–12 minutes with a partner)

Part 1 (Personal questions)

What is being tested?

Part 1 tests your ability to answer questions and give information about yourself. You will speak to the examiner. You will not need to speak to your partner.

What do you have to do?

- Spell your name, or part of your name, at the beginning of the exam.
- Answer the examiner's questions about yourself.
- This part of the exam lasts for 2–3 minutes.

Strategy

1 Be prepared to spell your name, or part of your name.
2 Listen to the examiner's questions. If you don't hear or understand a question, ask the examiner to repeat it.
3 Answer the question and give one or two more pieces of information. Do not give long, prepared answers.
4 Try to get a good balance between fluency, grammar and vocabulary.

Part 2 (Simulated situation)

What is being tested?

Part 2 tests your ability to talk with your partner and give ideas and opinions, make suggestions and come to an agreement.

What do you have to do?

- The examiner will give you a sheet of paper with pictures on it, and describe a situation.
- With your partner, you must discuss the situation using the pictures to help you, and come to an agreement.
- This part of the exam lasts for 2–3 minutes.

Strategy

1 Discuss each picture before making your choice. If you make your choice too quickly, you will run out of things to discuss.
2 Interact with your partner. Give suggestions, recommendations and opinions. Listen carefully to what your partner says and comment on these ideas.
3 If your partner is quiet, encourage him/her to speak by asking questions (you won't lose marks if your partner doesn't answer).
4 Summarise your choice and reasons at the end.
5 Try to get a balance between grammar, vocabulary and pronunciation, and interact well with your partner.

Part 3 (Extended turn)

What is being tested?

Part 3 tests your ability to describe a photograph using appropriate language, and organise your language when you speak for a longer time.

What do you have to do?

- The examiner will give you a photograph of an everyday situation. You will speak for one minute, describing the photograph.
- Your partner will talk about a different photograph on a similar topic for one minute.

Strategy

1 First, summarise what is in the photo.
2 Describe what you can see in more detail, e.g. the place, people and objects. Use prepositions of place to say where things are in the photo.
3 If you don't know the correct word for something, use different words to explain what it is.
4 Try to get a balance between fluency and accuracy.

Part 4 (General conversation)

What is being tested?

Part 4 tests your ability to discuss a topic with your partner, discussing your likes/dislikes, experiences and opinions.

What do you have to do?

- The examiner will ask you to talk to your partner about the topic that was introduced in Part 3.
- This part of the exam lasts for 3 minutes.

Strategy

1 Listen carefully to the instructions. If you don't hear or understand, ask the examiner to repeat them.
2 Give your opinions and experiences of the topic. Talk about your likes and dislikes, and give reasons.
3 Listen and respond to your partner. Ask your partner questions about his/her opinions and experiences, and find out his/her reasons.
4 Make sure that you and your partner share the conversation equally. You should encourage a quiet partner to speak by asking questions, but you won't lose marks if your partner doesn't answer.
5 Try to interact well with your partner, and get a good balance between grammar, vocabulary and pronunciation.

Pearson Education Limited
Edinburgh Gate
Harlow
Essex CM20 2JE
England
and Associated Companies throughout the world.

www.pearsonELT.com

© Pearson Education Limited 2013

First published 2015

ISBN: 978-1-2921-2493-3

Set in Myriad Pro
Printed in China (GCC/01)

Acknowledgements
The publishers and authors would like to thank the following people and institutions for their feedback and comments during the development of the material: Daniela Donati (Italy), Diana Pena (Mexico), Michael Smith (Spain), Pauline Bokhari, Pat Chappell, Sue Ireland (UK).

Author Acknowledgements
The authors would like to thank everyone at Bell for their support, Sue Ireland for her helpful suggestions, Cesar, Elliot and Alex for their love and support, and all the team at Pearson for their hard work and dedication.

We are grateful to the following for permission to reproduce copyright material:

Text
Article 1.1 adapted from http://www.guardian.co.uk/lifeandstyle/2009/oct/24/change-your-life-names-oliver-burkeman, Guardian News & Media Ltd 2009; Article 1.2 adapted from http://www.telegraph.co.uk/news/8489547/Happiness-the-5-big-personality-traits-which-one-are-you.html, copyright (c) Telegraph Media Group Limited; Article 1.3 adapted from www.mirror.co.uk/news/top-stories/2008/10/06/what-does-your-facebook-profile-say-about-you-115875-20778901/; Quote 1.4 from http://www.dailymail.co.uk/femail/article-1393619/Zoe-Kravitz-I-used-embarrassed-parents--I-steal-clothes.html#ixzz1jl8mSV24; Quote 1.6 from http://www.alicecooperechive.com/articles/index.php?showmag=sire&showart=080000 Originally published in Sirens of Cinema Vol 2 Issue 12, RAK Media Group, Inc.; Article 3.9 adapted from http://www.telegraph.co.uk/tecÚology/8679038/Debretts-guide-to-mobile-phone-etiquette.html, Debrett's Limited; Article 6.16 adapted from http://www.antimoon.com/learners/tomasz_szynalski_preinternet.htm, Tomasz P.Szynalski; Article 10.34 adapted from http://www.dailymail.co.uk/femail/article-1249709/Rise-metrosexual-Men-spend-longer-getting-ready-, Solo Syndication; Article 11.35 adapted from http://www.guardian.co.uk/world/2011/mar/25/indigenous-peoples-amazon-tourism-pressures, Guardian News and Media Ltd

In some instances we have been unable to trace the owners of copyright material, and we would appreciate any information that would enable us to do so.

The publisher would like to thank the following for their kind permission to reproduce their photographs:

(Key: b-bottom; c-centre; l-left; r-right; t-top)
akg-images Ltd: IAM 39; **Alamy Images:** Avesun 121 (camera), Steve Bloom Images 100, Buzz Pictures 98, Andre M. Chang 86, Corbis Premium RF 115/1, Design Pics Inc. 74, Fancy 89, Ian Francis 117 (an ice cube tray), David R. Frazier Photolibrary, Inc. 19b, Oliver Gerhard 103, Hemis 66, Richard Levine 115t, moodboard 46/5, Pick and Mix Images 115/4, Purestock 119b, Paul Springett 03 121 (space hopper), Paul Springett C 97, Robert Stainforth 47, Superstock 121 (torch), www.BibleLandPictures.com 34; **Corbis:** Atlantide Phototravel 21, Gerhard Egger 101, Paul Harris / JAI 96, Matilda Lindeblad / JoÚér Images 116t, Stephanie Maze 67, Alexander Porter / Image Source 12, Skyscan 80tl, Splash News 70, Luca Tettoni 65, Andrew Unangst 72, Mika Volkmann / dpa 43b, Roland Weihrauch / dpa 93; **En Motion Dance School, www.dance-en-motion.com:** 27, 27; **Getty Images:** Ata Mohammad Adnan 54, AFP 19t, 26, 42, 111, Phil Ashley 92, Julien Ballet-Baz Photography 102, Scott E Barbour 38b, Scott R Barbour 84, Steve Bloom 6t, Paul Bradbury 46/1, Melissa and Jackson Brandts 152, Pascal Broze 43t, Paul Burns 10/1, Yvette Cardozo 49, Cavan Images 10/4, Cultura / Zero Creatives 18, FilmMagic / Gregg DeGuire 118/A, Jac Depczyk 82, Digital Vision 25, Dkal Inc. 80/3, Miki Duisterhof / Photographer's Choice 16t, 16b, 116b, 119r, FilmMagic 13, Getty Images 117tr, Vladimir Godnik 9l, 114, Eleonora Grasso Photography 10/3, Robert Harding Productions 46l, Gavin Hellier 32, Jack Hollingsworth 121 (boy), Image Source 46/2, Coneyl Jay 7, Jupiterimages 85, Ray Kachatorian 10/5, JoÚ P Kelly 63r, David Malan 52, 80/5, Manchan 90, Ebby May 46/4, Ryan McVay 120t, Thorsten Milse 106, Cultura / Seb Oliver 80/2, Jose Luis Pelaez Inc 45, Simon Potter 46/3, Eric Raptosh Photography 57, Jay Reilly 9r, Andrew Rich 71, 105, rolfo 30t, David Sacks 28, Jay B Sauceda 80/4, Kalle Singer 55, Paul Souders 80cl, Peter H. Sprosty 110, Kazuhiro Tanda 10/2, Penny Tweedie 15l, VI-Images via Getty Images 24, K. Vukovich 60, Mark Warren Photography 80/1, Brad Wenner 10l, Mel Yates 119t, Chu Yong 108r; **By kind permission of Lee Hadwin/www.leehadwin.me:** 78, 79; **Monty Kerr:** 87; **Mary Evans Picture Library:** 38t; **nisyndication.com:** The Sun / NI Syndication 31; **Pearson Italia:** 50; **Seth Poppel Yearbook Library:** Seth Poppel Yearbook Library 37l, 37cl, 37cr, 37r; **Press Association Images:** Darren Calabrese / The Canadian Press 68, Huang Shaokui / Color China Photo / AP Images 104; **Rex Features:** Sam Barcroft 121 (lion pet), Col Pics / Everett 69, Gaza Press 15r, ITV 73, Alex Macnaughton 63l, Royal Caribbean 61, Sipa Press 118/B, Startraks Photo 118/C, 118/D; **Shutterstock.com:** CREATISTA 30b, Mike Flippo 117 (hose), Garry L. 121 (headphones), Gavran333 117 (spaghetti spoon), grafoto 120b, Mark Herreid 117 (secateurs), objectsforall 117 (goggles), photopixel 117 (coffee maker), Poznyakov 14, RTimages 115/3, saiko3p 115/2, Donald R. Swartz 117 (lantern); **TopFoto:** © National Pictures 108l; **Helen Wyllie :** 20t, 20c, 20b, 117/A, 117/B, 117/C, 118 (mushroom), 118 (onion), 118 (raspberry), 118 (tomato), 122/A, 122/B, 122/C, 122/D; **Yonhap News Agency:** 56

All other images © Pearson Education

In some instances we have been unable to trace the owners of copyright material, and we would appreciate any information that would enable us to do so.

Illustrated by Oxford Designers and Illustrators

Every effort has been made to chase the copyright holders and we apologise in advance for any unintentional omissions. We would be pleased to insert the appropriate acknowledgement in any subsequent edition of this publication.